A "Most Censored" Story....

-Project Censored

"Fitrakis & Wasserman are the Woodward & Bernstein of the 2004 Election."

-Rev. Jesse Jackson

Essential Documents on the 2004 Election
767 pages. From CICJ Books/Freepress.org

DID GEORGE W. BUSH STEAL AMERICA'S 2004 ELECTION?

Essential Documents

Edited by Bob Fitrakis, Steve Rosenfeld and Harvey Wasserman

Preface by Rev. Jesse Jackson

INCLUDES THE CONYERS REPORT

Coming in the Spring of 2006 from the New Press:
"What Happened in Ohio"
Edited by Bob Fitrakis, Steve Rosenfeld & Harvey Wasserman

BE KNOWN... ONLY BY SILENCE WILL WE BE DEFEATED

"What no one seemed to notice... was the ever widening gap... between the government and the people...

"And it became always wider... the whole process of its coming into being, was above all diverting, it provided an excuse not to think for people who did not want to think anyway... (it gave us some dreadful, fundamental things to think about... and kept us so busy with continuous changes and 'crises' and so fascinated... by the machinations of the 'national enemies,' without and within, that we had not time to think about these dreadful things that were growing, little by little, all around us...

"Each step was so small, so inconsequential, so well explained or, on occasion, 'regretted,' that unless one understood what the whole thing was in principle, what all these 'little measures'... must some day lead to, one no more saw it developing from day to day than a farmer in his field sees corn growing...

"Each act... is worse than the last, but only a little worse. You wait for the next and the next. You wait for one great shocking occasion, thinking that others, when such a shock comes, will join you in resisting somehow.

"You don't want to act, or even talk, alone...

"You don't want to 'go out of your way to make trouble.'

"But the one great shocking occasion, when tens or hundreds or thousands will join with you, never comes. That's the difficulty.

"The forms are all there, all untouched, all reassuring, the houses, the shops, the jobs, the mealtimes, the visits, the concerts, the cinema, the holidays.

"But the spirit, which you never noticed because you made the lifelong mistake of identifying it with the forms, is changed.

"Now you live in a world of hate and fear, and the people who hate and fear do not even know it themselves.

"When everyone is transformed, no one is transformed...

"You have accepted things you would not have accepted five years ago, a year ago, things your father... could never have imagined."

From Milton Mayer, *They Thought They Were Free, The Germans, 1938-45*
(Chicago: University of Chicago Press, 1955)

BOB FITRAKIS & HARVEY WASSERMAN have been at the core of Ohio's stolen 2004 election story since long before it happened.

Fitrakis is publisher and editor of the Columbus Free Press and www.Freepress.org. Wasserman is senior editor and columnist. Based in central Ohio, their ground zero crisis coverage built a substantial internet following in the lead-up to Ohio's 2004 election.

Their *Diebold's Political Machine*, running at MotherJones.Com on March 5, 2004, predicted major problems with Ohio's voting machines eight months before the balloting.

On October 27, 2004, a week before the November 2 election, their "Twelve Ways Bush is Now Stealing the Ohio Vote" helped drive the Freepress.org, circulation up to 50,000 visits/day, with wide re-circulation through other websites and into the mainstream media.

Reporting directly from their home town neighborhoods, Fitrakis & Wasserman worked through the election cycle to expose the intimidation, disenfranchisement, fraud and vote theft that defined the Ohio balloting.

On November 15 and 17, the Columbus Institute for Contemporary Journalism, Free Press' parent organization, convened public hearings where local citizens could put their stories on the record, under oath.

Moderated by Fitrakis, the hearings drew worldwide media coverage. Reverend Jesse Jackson then helped spark a national movement around what happened in Ohio. Congressman John Conyers followed with forums in Washington and at Columbus City Hall. The resulting report by the staff of U.S. Rep. John Conyers, "What Went Wrong in Ohio?" substantiated the Freepress.org findings, now backed by hundreds of affidavits from disenfranchised Ohio voters.

On January 6, 2005, a booming grassroots election protection movement fed America's first Congressional challenge to a state's presidential electors.

Fitrakis & Wasserman continue their unique coverage of the escalating 2004 election scandal and the GOP attempts to do more of the same in 2008. With Steve Rosenfeld, they have compiled *Did George W. Bush Steal America's 2004 Election: Essential Documents*, the definitive documentary sourcebook from www. Freepress.org. Their next book with Rosenfeld will be published by The New Press in Spring 2006.

Here, *How the GOP Stole America's 2004 Election & Is Rigging 2008* presents an "executive summary" of bullet points based on Fitrakis & Wasserman's ground zero coverage. This is the essential core digest of shattering electoral events that continue to change America at its very heart.

How The GOP Stole America's 2004 Election & Is Rigging 2008

by
Bob Fitrakis & Harvey Wasserman

www.Freepress.org / CICJ Books / www.harveywasserman.com

DEDICATION

This is dedicated to Bill Moss
and to all those who fight for freedom, dignity and voters' rights.

How the GOP Stole America's 2004 Election & Is Rigging 2008

By Bob Fitrakis and Harvey Wasserman Copyright c 2005 by Bob Fitrakis and Harvey Wasserman
All Rights Reserved

Published by CICJ Books/www.Freepress.org
1240 Bryden Road; Columbus, OH 43205
in conjunction with
www. harveywasserman. com
Box 09683; Bexley, OH 43209

Designed and set by Charlie Einhorn, Adam Einhorn and Harvey Wasserman.

The Columbus Institute for Contemporary Journalism is a 501(C)(3) non-profit organization.

ISBN # 0-9753402-8-X

PREFACE:

The election of 2004 was stolen, most crucially in Ohio. This book shows some of how it was done, and some of how the GOP is already locking up the 2008 election.

Ohio Secretary of State J. Kenneth Blackwell was the Republican Party's point man in 2004's most crucial swing state. Through him the GOP used a "do everything" strategy involving many different undemocratic, dishonest and often illegal—but extremely effective—techniques to steal enough votes from John Kerry to thwart the will of the people and put Bush back in the White House.

The official count of 5,625,632 Ohio votes shows George W. Bush winning the state by 118,775 votes. In fact he lost it by at least that much.

The official vote count shows George W. Bush winning the popular vote nationwide by about three million votes. In fact he lost it by about 1.5 million.

The Electoral College gave Bush the presidency by a vote of 286 to 251. But based on Ohio alone, Bush should have lost 266 to 271. If exit polls in Iowa, New Mexico and Nevada are also given their due, Bush should have lost to Kerry by 251 to 286.

This book focuses primarily—but not entirely—on Ohio. It only scratches the surface as to what was done to change the outcome of this election here. New evidence is surfacing even as we compile this. More will surely emerge over the years to come.

As reporters deeply rooted in central Ohio, we watched the election unfold before our eyes and under our feet. Co-author Harvey Wasserman grew up in one of the districts in which the election violations were most obscene; co-author Bob Fitrakis now lives in it.

Many months in advance, we unhappily predicted much of what ultimately did unfold.

In this short book we have laid out much of what we have found as clearly and simply as possible. We've provided sources and references for those of you who wish to dig deeper. We have based much of this book on documents appearing in *Did George W. Bush Steal America's 2004 Election?* (CICJ Books), which we compiled with Steve Rosenfeld. In a sense, this serves as an executive summary of that 767-page volume.

We've also included coverage of just a few of the irregularities that have surfaced in Florida, New Mexico and Nevada. We believe it is highly likely that as much was done in those states to shift the 2004 outcome as in Ohio. Far more research needs to be done there and in other key swing states.

This slim volume could have been exponentially larger. Even as we go to press, the Governor of Ohio has pleaded no contest to unprecedented misdemeanor ethics charges that are thoroughly intertwined with the theft of Ohio's 2004 election. Serious allegations have also surfaced about possible misallocation of many millions of federal HAVA dollars. If proven even partially true, these charges could reshape the public view of Ohio's 2004 election.

At best, it will be years before this is all sorted out.

To the best of our abilities, everything in this book is factual and fully documented. As mentioned it is of necessity a work in progress. In many cases, we merely cite occurrences without judgement or further analysis. At this stage of history, it is the pattern of events that may be of most significance.

Taken in isolation, there may certainly be "explanations" for much of what happened in Ohio and elsewhere during the election of 2004. There will also be many who dismiss factors such as exit polls or long lines at voting stations as being insignificant or irrelevant.

But we believe what is presented in this digest is the tip of the iceberg. We are still very early in the process of getting to the bottom of what really happened during this election. If history is any indicator, there is far more yet to come out.

At this point, we believe it all leads to one inescapable conclusion. We invite you to see for yourself.

—Bob Fitrakis & Harvey Wasserman - Autumn 2005; Columbus, Ohio

CONTENTS:

PART ONE:

HOW THE GOP STOLE
AMERICA'S 2004 ELECTION

Chapter One

The Set-Up

1. *In defiance of long-standing, universally accepted international practice, Ohio election officials denied routine polling station access to certified observers from the United Nations, independent international election protection teams and American non-governmental organizations.*

Every meaningful election in the world today is subject to international monitoring, either by the United Nations, or by independent teams from various countries, or from non-governmental organizations, or by all of the above.

The United States throughout its history has worked in various ways to "bring democracy" to other countries. Most recently, the Bush Administration has, since 2003, waged a bloody, destructive war to "bring democracy to Iraq."

Presidential elections in Ukraine in 2004, just prior to the U.S. presidential elections, were subjected to the kind of international scrutiny now expected in due course in every country if they are to be given any credence. Due to abuses, intimidation, theft and fraud by the incumbent, and based on evidence from the monitoring process and, most importantly, from exit polling (more on that later), the elections were overturned and a re-vote was forced. As a result, the incumbent who allegedly won the first election was declared the loser in the second, and was thrown out of office.

The global consensus about this pair of Ukrainian elections was that the result of the second election was the fair, right and democratic outcome. This stunning victory for the persistence of faith in democracy would not have been possible without full access to the voting and exit polling process being guaranteed to international monitors.

A co-author of this book, Bob Fitrakis, served as an international election observer in El Salvador in 1994. In that instance, the United Nations guaranteed access to the polls, along with a wide range of international bodies. The abundance of armed governmental troops and guerrillas throughout the country made the situation tense. Only the observers' presence gave the election meaning.

Throughout the former Soviet Union, the much-heralded "fall of communism" has also been accompanied by intense election scrutiny by the UN and others. The world has agreed that through the use of international monitors, we should no longer be forced to hear the cynical words of the dictator Josef Stalin: "It matters not who casts the votes, only who counts them."

So elections in the former Soviet Union have also been closely watched. In concert with exit polling from highly advanced experts such as Warren Mitofsky, the father of exit polling, the monitoring of popular elections has become an exact science.

Exit polls are normally considered to be extremely accurate, especially with large sample sizes. The margin of error in recent German national elections has been as low as plus/minus 0.01 percent. Exit polls have been equally accurate in predicting elections in Great Britain and, of course, in exposing a fraudulent election in Ukraine. In the American 2004 national election, pollster Warren Mitofsky issued an error margin of plus/minus 1.0 percent, later adjusted to 1.1 percent based on a reduced sample size. (As discussed later in this book, official vote counts varied from exit polls in ten key swing states by margins far in excess of the standard error factor, a virtual statistical impossibility that casts doubt on who really won the 2004 election).

In today's world, no credibility can be attached to any election that is not conducted under the watchful eye of established independent observers, and certified with the use of computerized exit polling.

Except, apparently, in the United States. And most particularly in Ohio in 2004.

Prior to America's 2004 election, Cuban President Fidel Castro offered to send monitors to make sure the US vote was fairly administered. The U.S. media treated Castro's offer as a joke. The Cuban dictator does not himself allow monitors to observe the elections in his country.

But then American officials followed in Castro's footsteps. In the lead-up to the 2004 elections, numerous independent and non-governmental organizations requested permission from Ohio election officials to gain access to polling stations for routine observation and monitoring, as in Iraq and Ukraine.

These requests were uniformly rejected. Without public explanation, Ohio Secretary of State J. Kenneth Blackwell refused all requests from non-partisan national and international organizations to establish impartial observation and monitoring procedures during the Ohio 2004 election.

Co-author and El Salvador election observer Bob Fitrakis was personally present in a meeting in which Matt Damschroder, former chair of the Franklin County Republican Party and Director of the Franklin County (Columbus) Board of Elections, denied international monitoring groups the right to observe the Ohio elections. Among other things, Damschroder warned that if they set foot within 100 feet of polling places in Franklin County, he would have them arrested.

Throughout the rest of the world, such an edict would be viewed as an admission of intent to steal an election. The United Nations and other election protection organizations would see Ohio's actions as the core definition of a renegade dictatorship. The Bush Administration made it clear in Ukraine that such behavior would not be tolerated.

With the denial of access to international monitors, Ohio's 2004 election would generally be considered a "demonstration election," a meaningless show for a repressive regime. By international standards, it had no more credibility in the eyes of history or the world than one in Castro's Cuba, the former Soviet Union or any of scores of dictatorships where elections, presidential and otherwise, are mere window dressings, with a predetermined outcome and an electorate deprived of its rights.

Secretary of State Blackwell, Director Damschroder and other administrators have never issued a written explanation as to why the international observers were banned from Ohio's polling places.

After Ohio's election, in further violation of internationally accepted procedure, and of American election law, Blackwell ordered that all tally sheets and other crucial documents pertaining to the presidential vote be locked down. As we write, public access to those records is still being denied. One specific instance of a denial of access is cited later in this book.

NOTES:

The refusal of the Ohio Secretary of State's Office to allow international observers into polling places was confirmed by Franklin County Board of Elections Director Matt Damshroder in an August 2004 meeting attended by co-author Bob Fitrakis, Attorney Susan Truitt of Citizens Active for Secure Elections (CASE), international election observers and some twenty others at Damschroder's office in Columbus.

The refusal was reported in the *Columbus Dispatch* and a wide range of other publications. It is also cited in:

U.S. House Judiciary Committee Democratic Staff Report, "Preserving Democracy: What Went Wrong in Ohio," January 5, 2005. Hereafter referred to as *Conyers Report*. A copy of this report appears in:

Bob Fitrakis, Steve Rosenfeld & Harvey Wasserman, editors, "Did George W. Bush Steal America's 2004 Election?: Essential Documents," CICJ Press (Columbus: 2004), hereafter referred to as: *Essential Documents*.

Much material in this book also comes from the public hearings sponsored by the Columbus Institute for Contemporary Journalism. The public hearing held at New Faith Baptist Church on Saturday, November 13, 2004, can be accessed at http://Freepress.org/images/departments/4254PublicHearing.txt.

The public hearing at the Franklin County Courthouse, Monday, November 15, 2004, can be accessed at http://Freepress.org/images/departments/4263PublicHearing.txt . These two initial hearings will be referred to as *CICJ Hearing Transcripts*, and can be accessed at http://Freepress.org/departments/display/19/2004/983 .

Byron Dierk, "Election Intervention: United Nations, Others Must Observe U.S. Process, *Manitou Messenger*, October 15, 2004.

2. While international observers were banned from Ohio polling stations, partisan "challengers" were welcomed by the Ohio Secretary of State into vantage points in the election process that many believed were threatening, disruptive and disenfranchising, especially to minority groups who voted predominantly Democratic.

While the Secretary of State and local Republican officials banned international observers from Ohio polling stations, they did allow in partisan "challengers" who got access to the actual registration tables within those polling stations.

Prior to the election, the Republican Party announced that it would deploy ten thousand of its activists and attorneys to be stationed inside the voting stations, with the intent of questioning those who came to vote. The GOP made clear its intent to focus these activists on inner city precincts where the vast majority of voters would be African-American. The Democrats countered with some three thousand challengers of their own, pledged not to challenge voters, but to counter Republican challenges.

Ohio's Secretary of State ruled that, unlike the nonpartisan international observers, such partisan challengers would be welcomed.

Democratic challengers were also given access. But Democrats argued that the purpose of allowing in the challengers was to delay the voting process in heavily Democratic precincts, thus lengthening the lines and making it difficult for inner-city citizens to wait out the vote.

As sworn testimony later indicated, these fears were realized: the challengers added to the chaos and delays that further paralyzed inner-city precincts that were suspiciously short of voting machines, and from which tens of thousands of citizens turned away without voting. The *Washington Post* estimated that in the city of Columbus alone, some 15,000 to 20,000 would-be voters turned away from the polls rather than braving the long lines. A study by the Democratic Party later estimated that a full three percent of the state's potential voters turned away because of the lines, meaning more than 170,000 Ohioans did not vote because of them—a number far in excess of Bush's official margin of victory.

The Democrats and voting rights groups challenged the presence of challengers, winning a number of court battles but losing out on the eve of the election. By all accounts a substantial number of Republican challengers did gain access to a number of inner city precincts and did contribute to delays and to an atmosphere of intimidation.

A later Congressional investigation, conducted by U.S. Representative John Conyers (D-MI), charged that the GOP challengers played a "Jim Crow" role in the election reminiscent of the Ku Klux Klan in the post-Civil War South.

NOTES:

Reports of the impending intrusion of partisan challengers may have gotten their first widespread circulation in Bob Fitrakis' and Harvey Wasserman's, "Twelve Ways Bush is Now Stealing the Ohio Vote," www.commondreams.org, October 27, 2004. It appears in *Essential Documents*, p. 12.

Conyers Report, op. cit.

Ray Beckerman, "Basic Report from Columbus," www.Freepress.org, November 5, 2005. Appears in *Essential Documents*, p. 17.

Moss, et. al. v. Bush, et. al., "Original Action to Contest Election in the Supreme Court of Ohio," Case No. 04-2088. Filed, December 13, 2004, re-filed December 17, 2004. Hereafter referred to as *Moss v. Bush.*

3. The election was administered by an outspoken partisan activist with a clear personal stake in the outcome.

The official administrator of Ohio's 2004 presidential election was J. Kenneth Blackwell, Ohio's Secretary of State.

Blackwell simultaneously served as co-chair of the Committee to Re-elect George W. Bush and Dick Cheney.

In other words, the Ohio election, which decided the outcome of America's presidential race, was run by a partisan with a clear, obvious and explicit stake in the outcome of the election, and an oft-stated belief that God had anointed him to do so. Blackwell often compares himself to Martin Luther King and Mahatma Ghandi.

Like the barring of international observers, this was not an arrangement embraced with great credibility by a world community committed to fair elections, and could not have passed muster in, Iraq or Ukraine, 2005.

The Ohio situation replicated that of Florida 2000. Florida's then-Secretary of State Katherine Harris administered that election. Like Blackwell, she simultaneously served as co-chair of the state's committee to elect Bush and Cheney. After weeks of bitter controversy, it was Harris who made the key decisions that—backed by the U.S. Supreme Court—stopped a recount and gave the election to George W. Bush. Harris was later rewarded with a safe Congressional seat and is now running for the U.S. Senate. Blackwell now seeks the governorship of Ohio.

The backlash from the bitterly contested 2000 election is still very much a part of the American legacy. A major study by People for the American Way and the National Association for the Advancement of Colored People estimates that nationwide in 2000, in an election decided in Florida by a few hundred votes, some four million American voters were disenfranchised due to "illegal actions and incompetence by public officials, as well as outdated machines and inadequate voter education."

Blackwell served as a key Bush advisor in the Florida 2000 election. His presence there was widely reported in mainstream media accounts of the epic crisis.

Throughout the 2004 election, Blackwell repeatedly defended his dual role as partisan and administrator. He argued forcefully that he could be trusted to run a fair election despite his personal stake in it.

But throughout the campaign Blackwell aggressively raised money for Bush-Cheney.

Blackwell used his position as Secretary of State to propose language, approve the ballot, certify petition signatures, and actively campaign for passage of Issue One, a Constitutional Amendment banning gay marriage in Ohio (Issue One also did away with spousal benefits for unmarried couples with at least one partner working for a governmental agency).

Issue One was widely viewed as a means to enhance Republican chances by tapping into the state's right-wing fundamentalist community, of which Blackwell is an outspoken leader. Polls showed that 80% of those supporting Issue One also backed Bush.

Soon after the election, Blackwell issued a fundraising letter that claimed credit for delivering Ohio to George W. Bush. The letter raised serious controversy in part because many Ohioans believe Blackwell delivered the state not through above-board political campaigning, but by the dishonest misuse of his position as election administrator. (In that same letter, Blackwell illegally solicited corporate contributions; he later admitted the illegality, allegedly withdrew the request, and was not prosecuted).

After the election, Blackwell published an-op ed in the *Washington Times*, a Republican-owned newspaper controlled by the right-wing extremist, Minister Sun Myung-Moon, entitled "How Ohio Pulled it Off." He lauded his own performance in administering the 2004 Ohio balloting. The outcome, he said, was a "great success."

But civil rights activist Rev. Jesse Jackson likened Blackwell's dual role as partisan and administrator to "the fox watching the chicken house." It was, he said, like having the owner of a football team referee his own team's games.

Blackwell refused to appear for all scheduled depositions in lawsuits filed with the Ohio Supreme Court in re: his administration of the election.

Blackwell also refused to testify in Washington in front of a Congressional committee chaired by fellow Republican Bob Ney (R-OH). On March 22, 2005, Ney brought his committee to the statehouse in Columbus, where Blackwell did finally speak in front of Congresswoman Juanita Millender-McDonald (D-CA), Congresswoman Stephanie Tubbs Jones (D-OH), and Ney himself.

Blackwell's talk with Ney went reasonably smoothly. But in the course of his testimony, Blackwell turned his back on Rep. Millender-McDonald, about which she complained bitterly. His now-infamous dialog with Rep. Jones turned exceedingly hostile.

Soon after the election, America's national organization of Secretaries of Sate evaluated the practice of elections being administered by partisan officials with a clear stake in their outcome. The Secretaries opted to allow the practice to continue.

In the eyes of the democratic world, the administration of elections by partisan officials invested in the outcome is a no-brainer. No election so run can be considered credible.

In November 2005, Ohio voters will weigh in on a Constitutional Amendment designed to ban such a situation (more on that later).

But both the elections in Florida 2000 and Ohio 2004 enter history as ones that were run by Secretaries of State who had a clear, outspoken interest in how they turned out. In both cases, amidst epic firestorms of controversy and dispute, the candidate favored by those administering the elections somehow won…and went on to become president of the United States.

In neither case, given the way these elections were administered, would the world community have considered them fair, balanced, or acceptable.

NOTES:

J. Kenneth Blackwell, Secretary of State of Ohio, to Robert Bennett, Chairperson, Cuyahoga County Board of Elections, October 5, 2004. This letter appears in "Essential Documents."

Bob Fitrakis & Harvey Wasserman, "How a Republican Election Supervisor Manipulated the Vote, in Black and White," www.Freepress.org, November 23, 20-04. This article was voted one of the Most Censored Stories of 2004.

Fitrakis & Wasserman, "Twelve Ways Bush is Now Stealing the Ohio Vote," op. cit.

Jim Dao, "GOP Bid to Contest Registrations is Blocked," *New York Times*, October 28, 2004, p. A25.

Hilary Shelton, Statement, "Preserving Democracy – What Went Wrong in Ohio," Judiciary Democratic Forum, National Association for the Advancement of Colored People (December 8, 2004).

People for the American Way, and the National Association for the Advancement of Colored People, "The Long Shadow of Jim Crow: Voter Intimidation and Suppression in America Today," September, 2004. See www.pfaw.org, and www.naacp.org.

Alan Fram, "Dems May Challenge Electoral Vote Count," Associated Press, January 6, 2004.

3. Claims that Ohio's Election Boards were bi-partisan were compromised by the Secretary of State's legal authority to screen election board members before their appointments, to fire them at his discretion, and to break tie votes where boards were divided.

Amidst the bitter controversies that arose before, during and after Ohio's 2004 elections, the major media and many independent observers argued that there could be no theft of the election because its administration was allegedly bi-partisan. According to Ohio law, the election boards in the state's 88 counties had to be evenly divided between Democrats and Republicans. This effectively disenfranchised third parties. But it allegedly meant that representatives of the two major parties would balance each other out and guarantee that no illegalities would be tolerated.

But the bi-partisanship is a myth. The boards were indeed divided by party. But they were divided two-two, leaving Blackwell the power to break ties.

Moreover, outside of Ohio's major urban centers the Democratic Party hardly exists. The actual loyalties of the so-called Democrats in rural counties are often a matter of debate.

Furthermore, under Ohio law every individual served at the pleasure of the Republican Secretary of State, Kenneth Blackwell. Blackwell had the right to reject any nominee from either party. He also retained the power to remove any individual board member at any time, and, indeed to fire a whole board at once, if he desired.

On October 5, 2004, Blackwell threatened to do exactly that. In a letter to Robert Bennett, the Republican chair of the Cuyahoga County (Cleveland) Board of Elections, Blackwell warned that "failure to comply with my lawful directives will result in official action, which may include removal of the Board and its Director."

In fact, the edicts Blackwell issued in this particular letter reversed long-standing Ohio practices, and involved a hotly contested interpretation of how to use provisional ballots (more on that later). But Blackwell made it clear he would not hesitate to overrule the alleged bi-partisanship of any county election board if he so chose. He also had the power to break ties on votes in which the four-person boards of elections were split two-two. In the course of the election, Blackwell did not hesitate to break ties; after it, he threatened to fire at least one election board (Lucas County) in its entirety.

Furthermore, Blackwell reinterpreted the term "jurisdiction" for voting purposes under Ohio law. Historically, a provisional vote was counted if the vote was cast in the right county, since the county board of elections was viewed as having jurisdiction. But following Ohio's 2004 presidential primary, Blackwell changed the rules and decided that a provisional vote would only count if cast in the right precinct—now interpreted as having jurisdiction—as opposed to the right county. This ruling created tremendous confusion and contention before, during and after the 2004 presidential vote.

NOTES:

Blackwell to Bennett, op. cit.

J. Kenneth Blackwell, "Secretary of State J. Kenneth Blackwell's Findings and Remedies Regarding the Lucas County Board of Elections," www.sos.state.oh.us, May 28, 2005. Hereafter referred to as Blackwell, "Findings and Remedies."

Bob Fitrakis & Harvey Wasserman, "Did the GOP Steal Another Ohio Election?" www.commondreams.org, August 5, 2005. This article also appears under the title "Dramatic New Link Between Ohio's 'Coingate,' Voinovich Mob Connections, and the theft of the 2004 Election," www.Freepress.org, July 29, 2005.

Moss v. Bush, op. cit.

5. Claims that Ohio's 88 county election boards operated in a non-partisan or bi-partisan manner were compromised by the fact that the paid staffs of the election boards in two of Ohio's biggest counties—Franklin and Hamilton—were run by extremely partisan Republican Directors, as was also the case in a number of other key counties.

Though the bi-partisan nature of Ohio's 88 county election boards was compromised by the power of the Secretary of State to fire them, of more practical importance may have been the power of the Directors. Under Ohio law, the party that carried the previous gubernatorial election in a given county may claim the Director's position of that county's Board of Election until the next gubernatorial election. That is balanced by the losing party being given the Chair of the Board of Election, with the Vice-Chair position going to the winning party.

In Cuyahoga County, the state's biggest, the Democratic Party chose Michael Vu to fill the Director's position. The Cuyahoga Board of Elections chair was held by Robert Bennett, Chair of the Ohio Republican Party.

Though Vu was favored by the Democrats, he was generally viewed as a non-partisan technocrat who shied away from overt partisan favoritism. The GOP leveled no charges against him relating to any administrative errors in the 2004 election. In fact a number of outcomes in inner city Cleveland precincts went very much the Republicans' way. In some inner city precincts an extremist right-wing candidate received as much as forty percent of the vote, an unrealistic outcome.

In Franklin County, the Director's position went to Matt Damschroder, former chair of the county's Republican Party and an outspoken right wing activist.

NOTES:

Fitrakis & Wasserman, "How a Republican…", op. cit.

Fitrakis & Wasserman, "Twelve Ways…", op. cit.

6. Eleven months before the election, the Republican Director of the Franklin County Board of Elections, in his office, accepted a check from a lobbyist from the Diebold voting machine company.

On January 9, 2004, eleven months before the presidential election, Damschroder accepted a $10,000 check from Pasquale "Pat" Gallina in Damschroder's office at the Board of Elections.

Gallina was a contractor for the Diebold voting machine company. It was the day bids were opened for the county's purchases of voter registration software.

At Damschroder's request, Gallina made the check out to the Franklin County Republican Party, and handed it to Damschroder. Damschroder then mailed it to his party.

During the election, Damschroder made decisions on the allocation of voting machines and other crucial issues in ways widely believed to be meant to serve the Republican Party and help swing the outcome to George W. Bush.

It was Damschroder, for example, who made the crucial decisions about the allocation of voting machines, decisions that resulted in critical shortages at predominantly African-American inner-city precincts, resulting in long lines and extensive disenfranchisement.

Similar charges were raised against the Republican-appointed Director of the Hamilton County (Cincinnati) Board of Elections.

NOTES:

Doug Caruso, Joe Hallet & Robert Vitale, "Vendor's Donation Questioned," *Columbus Dispatch*, July 16, 2005, p. 1A.

Fitrakis & Wasserman, "Did the GOP Steal...?" op. cit.

7. A Diebold representative offered the Chair of the Athens County Board of Elections a $1000 contribution as the county was preparing to buy voting machines.

Susan Gwinn, head of the Athens County Democratic Party and chair of the Athens County Board of Elections, told the *Columbus Dispatch* that in October, 2003, William Chavanne offered her a $1000 donation to go to the party. At the time, the county was in the process of buying new voting machines. Gwinn refused the contribution. Chavanne said the offer had nothing to do with trying to influence the county's choice in what kind of machines to buy.

NOTES:

Jim Siegel, Robert Ruth & Robert Vitale, "Diebold's Reps' Tactics Criticized," *The Columbus Dispatch*, p. 1, August 14, 2005.

8. The Republican Director of the Hocking County Board of Elections raised money for the GOP in her office and improperly shredded voter registration documents.

In Hocking County, Lisa Schwartze, the Republican-appointed Director of the Board of Elections, used her position to raise funds for the county's Republican Party. According to reports from a staffer, Schwartze also illegally shredded several thousand official documents without formal approval from the Board of Elections.

When Deputy Director Sherole Eaton made Schwartze's actions public, Eaton was fired, and received no support from the BOE's Democratic members.

NOTES:

Victoria Parks, "My Report from Hocking County," www.Freepress.org., July 5, 2005.

Rep. John Conyers & Rep. Marcy Kaptur, letter to U.S. Attorney-General Alberto Gonzalez, August 8, 2005.

9. The Lucas County (Toledo) Board of Elections was chaired by Bernadette Noe, wife of Tom Noe, a Bush supporter indicted for money laundering and being investigated for stealing $4 million from the state of Ohio and for misappropriating $12.6 million of a $50 million state investment fund.

The Lucas County Board of Elections was chaired by Bernadette Noe, an outspoken Bush-Cheney advocate whose husband Tom was known as northwestern Ohio's "Mr. Republican," Tom Noe was also chair of the regional Bush-Cheney campaign.

In early 2004, Ms. Noe took over the BOE chair . Her husband, had served as Lucas County BOE chair from 1993 to 1998.

At this writing, Tom Noe has been indicted for illegal donations to the Bush-Cheney re-election campaign. Noe is charged with personally stealing $4 million from the Bureau of Workers Compensation, and for misappropriating another $12.6 million. Noe is the central figure in the "Coingate" scandal that also involves a bizarre rare coin fund in which Noe invested on behalf of the state.

(Partly as a result of his associations with Tom Noe, Gov. Robert Taft became the first sitting governor in Ohio history to be criminally sentenced with ethics violations. On August 18, 2005, Taft entered a no-contest plea to four first-degree misdemeanor charges in an Ohio court and was required to pay a nominal fine).

In the lead-up to the 2004 vote, on Election Day, and through the recount, the Noe's severely compromised public control over the election in Lucas County, that turned into one of the most chaotic and scandal-ridden in the state.

Under intense public fire, Ms. Noe announced her intention to resign in December, 2004. In April, 2005, a scathing report from the Ohio Secretary of State's office confirmed the assertions of voters within the county and by election protection advocates that widespread corruption and fraud under Ms. Noe's leadership almost certainly produced many thousands of votes being shifted to Bush and/or away from Kerry.

In April, Blackwell threatened to fire the entire Lucas County Board of Elections, which then resigned.

As of this writing, the Noes face a wide range of civil and potential criminal charges.

NOTES:

Blackwell, "Findings and Remedies," op. cit.

Conyers & Kaptur, letter to Gonzales, op. cit.

Fitrakis & Wasserman, "Did the GOP Steal....", op. cit.

Caruso et. al., "Vendor's Donation Questioned," op. cit.

Columbus Dispatch, Toledo Blade, Cleveland Plain-Dealer and others have widely reported on these incidents. See Chris Maag, "Breaking the Noe Story," *Columbus Monthly*, August, 2005, p. 129.

10. The Chair of the Lucas County Board of Elections was approached in a situation involving contributions from Diebold, and her husband made contributions that are being investigated.

In January, 2004, Bernadette Noe, Chair of the Lucas County Board of Elections, was approached by Pasquale "Pat" Gallina in a meeting in which Gallina offered what appeared to be a bribe on behalf of Diebold. Lucas County Elections Board Director Joe Kidd, who is now Gallina's attorney, was at the meeting.

Ms. Noe made public her concerns, which were eventually referred to U.S. Attorney Greg White. In the meantime, reports continue to surface that Ms. Noe's husband Tom, her predecessor as Chair of the Lucas County Board of Elections, may have made improper contributions to the GOP. The allegations are being investigated in concert with the "Coingate" scandal, including money laundering into the Bush campaign.

NOTES:

Julie Carr Smyth, "Probe Focuses on Donation to GOP, *Cleveland Plain-Dealer*, August 14, 2005.

See also: http://www.ohiohonestelections.org/

11. Overnight on October 11th-12th, 2004, three weeks prior to the November 2nd election, the headquarters of the Lucas County Democratic Party was burglarized, with the loss of crucial voter lists, internal correspondence and other sensitive campaign materials.

On the night of October 11th-12th, about three weeks prior to the November 2nd balloting, someone broke into the Toledo headquarters of the Lucas County Democratic Party. The alarm was not tripped. Three computers were taken, including the party's main unit. According to the *Toledo Blade*, the computers "contained highly sensitive information, including the party's financial information, names and personal phone numbers of hundreds of party members, candidates and volunteers."

The *Blade* also reported that the computers held many sensitive e-mails from candidates and party officials discussing strategy and other party business. Another computer, which belonged to an attorney, contained information on work to protect voters' rights.

The theft of the computers crippled the Democrats' get-out-the-vote campaign in northwestern Ohio, almost certainly costing the Kerry campaign thousands of votes. The perpetrators have never been found.

NOTES:

Fitrakis & Wasserman, "Did the GOP Steal....?", op. cit.

Richard Hayes Phillips, "The Phillips Report," December 31, 2004, appearing in *Essential Documents,* pp. 142-7. Hereafter known as "Phillips Report."

Associated Press, "Shades of Watergate! Lucas County Democratic Party Headquarters Burglarized," October 13, 2004.

Robin Erb, "Thieves Hit Democratic Party Offices: Computers Containing Sensitive Data Removed," *Toledo Blade*, October 13, 2004.

Richard Hayes Phillips, "Another Third-Rate Burglary," Freepress.org, December 25, 2004.

12. Sequoia touchscreen machines were brought into Lucas County in 2002 by Tom Noe, former Chair of the Board of Elections, now at the center of the "Coingate" scandals, but the county used Diebold opti-scan machines for the 2004 election.

In May, 2002, Lucas County Board Chair Tom Noe claimed credit for bringing Sequoia touchscreen voting counters into the county's tabulation process. Touchscreen machines that offer no paper trail or independent auditing capability are at the heart of nationwide controversy.

Other machines were tested in Lucas County. But on Election Day 2004 election, Lucas County opted for Diebold opti-scan machines.

NOTES:

Sequoia Press release, "Ohio County Completes the Nation's Fastest Installation of Touch Screen Voting Technology," May 10, 2002, appears at http://www.sequoiavote.com/mediadetail.php?id=57.

Blackboxvoting.org, op. cit.

Jim Drinkard, "High-tech Voting Accessory: Paper," *USA Today*, August 10, 2005, p. 8A.

13. Lucas County's Diebold machines broke down before Election Day, then were left in disrepair into Election Day, disenfranchising thousands.

Rather than the Sequoia machines installed by Noe, Lucas County operated with opti-scan machines from Diebold. Diebold principal Wally O'Dell, an avid Bush supporters, vowed to "deliver Ohio's electoral votes" to the GOP. Both Noe and O'Dell are major pioneer/ranger donors to George W. Bush.

In the weeks before the election, scores of Diebold machines froze up in tests. On Election Day, the Diebold machines in Toledo froze up again, disenfranchising thousands of inner-city voters.

NOTES:

Blackwell, "Findings and Remedies," op. cit.

Moss v. Bush, op. cit.

Phillips Report," op. cit.
Fitrakis & Wasserman, "Did the GOP Steal...?", op. cit.

Bob Fitrakis & Harvey Wasserman, "Diebold's Political Machine," www.MotherJones.com, March 5, 2005. This article appears in *Essential Documents*, p. 5.

14. Prior to Election Day, the Lucas County Board of Elections, chaired by Bernadette Noe, allowed GOP activists unsupervised access to unsecured ballots.

Before the November 2nd vote, the Lucas County BOE allowed GOP activists to have unsupervised access to unsecured Diebold opti-scan ballots. No such access was given to Democratic representatives.

The Lucas County BOE that made this decision was chaired by Bernadette Noe, wife of the chair of the northern Ohio Bush-Cheney Campaign. The decision to allow this access was severely criticized in a later report from the office of the Ohio Secretary of State.

NOTES:

"Moss v. Bush," op. cit.

Phillips Report," op. cit.

Blackwell, "Findings and Remedies," op. cit.

Fitrakis & Wasserman, "Did the GOP Steal...?", op. cit.

15. General disorganization and a wide range of administrative problems impaired the preparation for the vote in Lucas County, prompting a state investigation and the eventual resignation of the entire Board of Elections.

Under the chair of Bernadette Noe, an extraordinary set of problems plagued the lead-up to the November 2nd vote. Among the problems that surfaced in Lucas County, as cited by a later report from the Ohio Secretary of State, were the failure to maintain ballot security, failure to implement a tracking system for voter registration, issuance of incorrect absentee ballot forms, problems in removing the names of Ralph Nader and Peter Camejo from the ballot, failure to properly issue hospital ballots as prescribed by law, failure to maintain poll books, failure to examine campaign finance reports, and more.

The campaign finance issue became crucial later as it may have involved donations from former Lucas BOE Chair Tom Noe to the Bush-Cheney campaign, of which he was regional co-chair.

NOTES:

Moss v. Bush, op cit.

Blackwell, "Findings and Remedies," op. cit.

Phillips Report," op. cit.

Fitrakis & Wasserman, "Did the GOP Steal…?", op. cit.

Fitrakis & Wasserman, "Diebold's Political Machine," op. cit.

16. *George W. Bush's margin of victory for Ohio and thus for the presidency could be accounted for on voting machines owned, programmed and operated by partisan Republicans, one of whom was a personal friend who pledged, in a fundraising letter, to deliver the state's electoral votes to Bush.*

About 15% of the 5.6 million votes cast in the Ohio election were recorded by electronic voting machines that had no paper trails and could not be reliably monitored or recounted. This represented about 700,000 votes in an election whose official margin for George W. Bush was 118,775 votes. The reversal of a small percentage of the votes cast on electronic machines could have changed the outcome of the election. A shift of a mere six votes in each of Ohio's 11,000-plus precincts would have given Kerry the White House.

This 15% figure does not include electronic tabulating machines and other devices used to count paper and punch card ballots. But like the electronic DRE machines, on which votes were cast directly into a computer's memory bank, virtually all the voting machines used in Ohio were manufactured by companies with powerful, aggressively partisan Republican ownership.

Most notorious was Diebold, the Canton-based business machine giant. Diebold's chief player is Walden "Wally" O'Dell. In 2003, O'Dell visited George W. Bush's converted pig farm in Crawford, Texas, and returned as a Pioneer or Ranger who had raised more than $100,000 for Bush's campaigns. O'Dell soon hosted a fundraiser whose admission price was $1,000 per head. He also issued a fundraising letter in which he promised to deliver the state to Bush.

The letter raised howls of outrage as O'Dell's Diebold machines would control enough ballots in the 2004 election to tip the balance to George W. Bush, as O'Dell had promised. Diebold's General Election Management Systems software (GEMS).

The same was true of electronic machines provided by ES&S, Hart InterCivic, Triad and Sequoia.

ES&S is controlled in part by a company in which Sen. Chuck Hagel (R-NE) holds an ownership interest. Despite never having held elected to public office beforehand, Hagel was elected to the U.S. Senate from Nebraska twice (1996 and 2002) with the deciding votes being cast on machines in which he owned a part interest. In both cases, the actual outcomes were bitterly contested by serious students of Nebraska voting trends.

Relations between top management at ES&S and Diebold have been close dating from their early development, when a pair of brothers—Bob and Todd Urosevich—helped develop the software at both companies.

Hart InterCivic and Triad also have close Republican ties. After the November 2nd general election, Triad was charged with meddling with Ohio machines before the votes cast on them could be re-counted. It is in corporate affiliation with the company that provided Florida's Palm Beach County with the infamous butterfly ballots that helped give Bush the 2000 elections.

Serious post-election challenges erupted not just with the DREs, but with optical scan and other electronic devices that handled more than enough votes to shift the outcome of Ohio's vote count and thus the presidency. In a conference call involving Rev. Jesse Jackson, John Kerry acknowledged that he had lost every precinct in New Mexico where the votes were counted with DRE touch-screen machines. The outcome was independent of the precincts' demographic, racial, ethnic, income level or historic partisan leanings, said Kerry. All that mattered, Stalin-style, was how the votes were counted.

The same pattern held true throughout Ohio: More than enough votes were cast and/or counted on machines owned, programmed and operated by GOP-controlled companies than were needed to carry the election.

In Mahoning County alone, 78 voters reported that when they pushed the touchscreen machine on John Kerry's name, the light switched to George W. Bush; only two voters testified that it went the other way.
NOTES:

For an overview of the issue of electronic voting machines, see www.blackboxvoting.org.

Fitrakis & Wasserman, "Diebold's Political Machine, " op. cit.

CICJ Hearing Transcripts, op. cit.

Judiciary Democratic 2004 Election Forum, December 13, 2004, Columbus, Ohio. Hereafter referred to as *Conyers Testimony*.

House Administrative Committee Field Hearing, Columbus, Ohio, March 21, 2005. Hereafter referred to as *Ney Testimony*.

The National Democratic Party, "Democracy at Risk: The 2004 Election in Ohio," DNC Voting Rights Institute (DC: 2005). See www.Democrats.org/vri/. Hereafter referred to as *DNC Report*.

Jonathan Riskind, "Democrats Criticize How Ohio Handled 2004 Election," *Columbus Dispatch*, June 23, 2005, p. C4.

17. *The machines on which the deciding votes were cast in Ohio and elsewhere were vulnerable to partisan pre-programming and to Election Day re-programming, tampering and vote shifting, and were never securely certified by independent agencies as voting commenced, or as it proceeded, or through the recount process.*

In the years following the disputed 2000 election, scores of political and computer-based researchers thoroughly vetted real and imagined problems with electronic voting machines. As Ohio 2004 approached, it became clear that a significant number of the machines deployed in Ohio and elsewhere could not and still cannot be vouchsafed to have delivered a result that was immune from partisan re-programming, tampering and vote shifting.

In any event—unlike gambling machines or gas pumps—there was no independent monitoring organization that inspected the machines and certified them to be secure from tampering as Ohio's balloting began, or as the recount was initiated.

As we shall see, numerous, often highly bizarre malfunctions demonstrated by these machines during and after the election gave the public ample reason to question the reliability of their performance.

Elsewhere, in one infamous public display, Bev Harris of blackboxvoting.com, a leading voting machine researcher and advocate, reprogrammed on live national television an allegedly secure Florida voting machine in 90 seconds, yielding an easily controlled outcome.

A wide range of experts on computer science and the nature of the machines deployed in Ohio and elsewhere have testified under oath that it would have been both possible and relatively easy to alter by remote control the outcome delivered by voting machines in districts that could have swung the election. The alterations could have been done through official access to central tabulation equipment, over phone lines, or even from electronic devices controlled in vehicles doing drive-bys at key polling stations on Election Day.

Prior to the Ohio election, numerous voting machines were delivered to Franklin County (Columbus) precincts weeks before Election Day. Security was insufficient at these precincts to prevent the machines from being tampered with, and there was no independent inspection to confirm that they were secure as the elections began, or through the day of polling, or in the aftermath, before and during the recount.

In fact, in at least two counties, computer technicians did make intrusions into voting tabulating devices after the balloting but prior to the completion of the recount. Many Ohio counties, refused requests for independent post-election inspection of the hardware on which the election was decided. Shelby County dismantled and discarded key equipment before a recount could be administered.

Taken as a whole, the voting machines on which more than 700,000 Ohioans cast their DRE electronic ballots were profoundly insecure. So were the electronic tabulation machines on which a majority of the state's 5.6 million ballots were counted, without the benefit of nonpartisan monitors or a reliable recount.

As mentioned, all were owned, programmed and operated by companies with clear Republican interests, with O'Dell's Diebold being the highest-profile. The scant 118,775 -vote official margin for George W. Bush falls well within the range of anyone with a desire to manipulate the outcome and/or with access to any number of electronic pathways which were relatively easy to obtain for a wide range of machines entrusted with enough votes to swing the state.

NOTES:

www.blackboxvoting.org, op. cit.

Blackwell, *Report,* op. cit.

Phillips Report," op. cit.

Fitrakis & Wasserman, "Did the Republicans....?", op. cit.

Fitrakis & Wasserman, "Diebold's Political Machine," op. cit.

DNC Report, op. cit.

---

18. *In Auglaize County, the Deputy Director of the Board of Elections resigned after he complained that a former employee of the voting machine company ES&S was given inappropriate access to voting machines prior to Election Day.*

In a letter dated October 21, 2004, Ken Nuss, the deputy director of the Auglaize County Board of Elections, charged that a former ES&S employee was violating election protocol by improperly using county electronic voting machines.

Upon making the complaint, Nuss was suspended from his job. He then resigned his position while formally charging that Joe McGinnis, a former ES&S worker, had been given unauthorized access to the county's tabulating machines and ballot-making machines on the weekend of October 16.

The incident, viewed as minor at the time, was a precursor to additional disputes over unauthorized access to electronic voting machines during and after the election.

NOTES:

Moss v. Bush, op. cit.

Fitrakis & Wasserman, "Twelve Ways...", op. cit.

19. *On the subject of voter registration, the Republican Secretary of State's unique, unprecedented requirement that forms be printed on 80-pound paper caused chaos in trying to register people to vote.*

In the wake of the epic confrontation over the presidential balloting in Florida 2000, and in light of complaints of restricted access to the registration process, Congress passed the Help America Vote Act (HAVA), meant to make it easier for citizens everywhere to vote. Among other things, HAVA mandated that the states ease registration requirements.

Kenneth Blackwell went in the opposite direction. Prior to the Ohio vote, in the middle of major Democratic registration drives, Blackwell announced that the state would require all new voter registration forms to be printed on 80-pound paper. All other applications would be rejected, he pronounced.

But thousands of forms on lighter paper weights had already been received by various Boards of Election. Thousands of others were in the mail when Blackwell made his announcement. The *Cleveland Plain Dealer*, the state's biggest newspaper, had printed forms in its daily paper that were obviously not on 80-pound stock.

Blackwell's edict caused tremendous chaos in the pre-election process and ultimately cost thousands of Ohioans their right to vote. Blackwell referred to an obscure statute to justify the policy. He also claimed the heavier paper was needed for machine processing, though many counties used twenty-pound paper for scanning purposes.

In the midst of the controversy, reporters from the *Columbus Dispatch* obtained voter registration forms from Blackwell's own office, and confirmed they were on sixty-pound paper, not eighty-pound as Blackwell was demanding.

County election officials of both parties were mystified and often outraged by the ruling. It appeared to be an arbitrary dictate with no substantial reason or precedent for it in Ohio law. Some election boards returned the voter registration forms sent in on lighter paper, asking them to try again.

But many election officials from both parties announced they would ignore Blackwell's decree. They argued the requirement for heavier paper would cost their counties very substantial sums in printing costs and would leave them and their voters in limbo as to what forms already in process would remain acceptable, if any.

Blackwell's demand was eventually overruled by the courts. But by then it had caused extreme confusion and chaos among hopeful new voters. Thousands were left unsure as to whether or not they were actually registered. Many who had already registered on lighter paper tried to register again on heavier forms—when they could get them—resulting in still more problems.

In studying the lead-up to the election, the special Congressional investigative team commissioned by Rep. Conyers concluded that Blackwell had demanded the 80-pound requirement as a method of creating confusion and disarray amidst a massive voter registration campaign being conducted by the Democrats.

By all accounts, Blackwell's strategy worked. The intense conflict and confusion he created through this and other policies in the lead-up to the election and at polling stations on Election Day caused thousands of likely Democratic voters to be deprived of access to a ballot.

NOTES:

CICJ Hearings Testimony, op. cit.

Conyers Testimony, op. cit.

Ney Testimony, op. cit.

Conyers Report, op. cit.

Moss v. Bush, op. cit.

Fitrakis & Wasserman, "Twelve Ways...," op. cit.

Additional reports appeared in the *New York Times, Columbus Dispatch, Toledo Blade. Cleveland Plain Dealer*, et. al.

20. "Caging" tactics in the registration process, both official and unofficial, may have deprived thousands of Ohioans of their right to vote.

According to sworn testimony given after the election, unidentified independent groups were active prior to the election, primarily in the inner cities, signing up potential voters as if to register them, then discarding their forms. When these citizens showed up to vote, they learned they were not officially registered, and were thus effectively disenfranchised.

Also according to sworn testimony taken after the election, one county sheriff visited some fifty registered voters to inquire about their voting status. The visits were viewed as a form of intimidation against voters who had registered Democratic.

Overall, these caging techniques may have disenfranchised tens of thousands of citizens, most of them African-Americans.

NOTES:

CICJ Hearings Testimony, op. cit.

Conyers Testimony, op. cit.

Ney Testimony, op. cit.

Fitrakis & Wasserman, "Twelve Ways...," op. cit.

Suzanne Hoholik, "Voters Report Fake Calls: Instructions to Change Polling Place Don't Come from Board of Elections," *Columbus Dispatch,* October 22, 2004.

"Lake County Board of Elections," "Urgent Advisory," October 22, 2004. This flier appears in *Essential Documents,* p. 19. The Lake County BOE may not have been the true author.

Jim Dao, "Big G.O.P. Bid to Challenge Voters at Polls in Key State," *New York Times,* October 23, 2004.

Jim Dao, "Officials Say Two Court Rulings Will Halt G.O.P. Challenges," *New York Times,* October 30, 2004.

21. On Provisional Balloting, Blackwell imposed restrictive policies in direct contradiction to HAVA and to established Ohio practices, in ways that had a partisan impact.

HAVA further mandated that the use of provisional ballots be expanded and access extended so that more Americans could vote more easily. Again, Blackwell went in the opposite direction, in ways that by all accounts disproportionately harmed the Democratic tally.

Provisional ballots are meant to allow voters who encounter a snag or irregularity at the voting station to cast a ballot pending clarification. In many cases the problem can stem from the voter having moved, or from the precinct itself having moved. In Ohio 2004, sworn testimony taken after the election indicates there were an enormous, inordinate number of Democratic voters whose registration files had been somehow corrupted.

Traditionally, in Ohio elections, anyone who reported to a polling station within his or her county of residence could obtain a provisional ballot. This was especially useful in heavily populated urban areas, where multiple precincts could be set up at tables in the same building, often right next to each other.

Thus if a voter got into the wrong line in his/her polling station and wound up at a table that was for a different precinct, that precinct would issue a provisional ballot rather than making the voter stand in another line. If a voter showed up at the wrong precinct altogether, s/he could still get a provisional ballot and proceed along with the needs of the day.

As Election Day approached, Blackwell announced a change: A voter who showed up at the wrong precinct, even in the correct county or the correct building, and even if the precincts were operating out of tables right next to each other, would not have the provisional ballot counted no matter what the circumstance.

In direct contradiction to HAVA and long-standing Ohio practice, Blackwell told county election board members he would fire anyone who said otherwise. In his October 5 letter to Cuyahoga County Election Board Chair Robert Bennett, a Republican, Blackwell accused the board of attempting to create chaos by saying it would accept provisional ballots from voters registered in a precinct other than the one in which they were trying to cast a ballot.

But when Election Day did arrive, chaos ensued in heavily Democratic inner-city precincts that had been denied sufficient voting machines, and whose registration rolls were in chaos. Both Democratic and Republican county election officials told a committee led by Congressman Bob Ney that Blackwell's own website had inaccurate information on it, much of it six months out of date as to precinct location.

Blackwell's restrictions on provisional balloting added immensely to the chaos and caused thousands of potential voters to be denied their right to vote. According to sworn testimony taken after the election, many of these were older voters who had lived at the same address and voted in the same precinct for decades. By Blackwell's order, many had both regular ballots and provisional ballots uncounted.

Amidst the chaos, 155,428 provisional ballots were officially noted as having been cast in Ohio 2004, about five times the number cast in Florida 2004, where more total votes were cast. The true number of provisional ballots cast in Ohio may have been even higher, as it appears many provisional ballots may have been summarily trashed soon after they were cast. According to Dr. Norman Robbins, an independent observer, provisional ballots cast in at least one Cleveland precinct were summarily pitched, nearly all of them cast by African-Americans.

Officially, at least 16,000 provisional ballots are confirmed as having been set aside. They remain uncounted. Some 65% of those uncounted ballots came from heavily Democratic precincts.

NOTES:

Ney Testimony.

Conyers Report, op. cit.

Phillips Report," op. cit.

Moss v. Bush, op. cit.

Darrel Rowland & Lee Leonard, "Federal Agency Distances Itself from Ohio Official," *Columbus Dispatch*, October 20, 2004, p. 1A.

New York Times, "Blaming the Messengers," Editorial Page, February 3, 2005.

22. To the restrictions on provisional balloting, Blackwell added a demand that voters include their birth date on the application form.

Blackwell's demand that voters include their birth date on the application form for provisional ballots resulted in tremendous confusion among the Boards of Elections. By some accounts this requirement was enforced at some precincts and not at others. It almost certainly resulted in the discarding of thousands of provisional ballots as voters reported failing to include their birth dates on forms which then may or may not have resulted in their provisional ballots being trashed.

NOTES:

CICJ Hearings Testimony, op. cit.

Conyers Report, op. cit.

Conyers Testimony, op. cit.

Fitrakis, "And so the sorting and discarding of Kerry votes begins," November 10, 2004, Freepress.org.

Ney Testimony, op. cit.

DNC Report, op. cit.

23. Blackwell's suit to restrict provisional balloting was joined by Tom Noe.

Prior to the election, Democrats sued Blackwell to force him to allow provisional ballots to be cast by voters in precincts other than the one in which they were registered. Blackwell's defense against that suit was joined by Tom Noe, former chair of the Lucas County Board of Elections, husband of the then-current chair. Noe is at the center of Ohio's multi-million-dollar Coingate scandal.

NOTES:

Blackwell, "Report," op. cit.

Fitrakis & Wasserman, "Did the Republicans Steal…?", op. cit.

See also http://moritzlaw.osu.edu/electionlaw/docs/sandusky/doc5

24. Many precincts were redrawn prior to the 2004 election, many of them illogically, and were wrongly identified on the Secretary of State's website, which was six months out-of-date on Election Day, causing widespread confusion and disenfranchisement.

The state moved many precincts prior to the 2004 election. Many were incorrectly labeled on the Secretary of State's official website, which was six months out-of-date as of Election Day. In Lucas County, precinct boundaries were never correctly drawn or finalized.

Many of the reassigned precinct lists were illogical in terms of where voters lived, with voters being switched from voting stations near their homes to ones far away.

Blackwell's restrictive edicts demanding that provisional ballots be accepted only in the voter's correct precinct meant that many who reported to the precinct location listed on the Secretary of State's website could not vote there and were also denied the ability to cast a provisional ballot by order of the same Secretary of State who inaccurately posted their precinct location.

In some cases, voters reported that their right to a provisional ballot was denied even though the table for their authorized precinct was right next to the one at which they were standing. It is also likely that some provisional ballots submitted at such tables were trashed. Voters also testified that some poll workers did not know how to issue provisional ballots.

According to sworn testimony taken after the election, this situation resulted in many such cases due to lines being unmarked or wrongly marked at polling stations.

It is unclear how many citizens were thus disenfranchised.

NOTES:

CICJ Hearings Testimony, op. cit.

Conyers Report, op. cit.

Conyers Testimony, op. cit.

Ney Testimony, op. cit.

DNC Report, op. cit.

25. From 2000 to 2004, Blackwell's Office of Secretary of State eliminated a large number of precincts in Lucas and other counties favorable to the Democrats, putting more voters into existing or redrawn precincts, making it ultimately harder for them to vote.

In the years prior to the 2004 election, the Secretary of State eliminated a large number of precincts in twenty counties favorable to the Democrats, and no counties favorable to the Republicans.

In Lucas County, the number of precincts went from 530 to 495 from November, 2003 to November, 2004. At the same time, the number of registered voters rose from 288,190 to 300,137.

The elimination of these precincts caused added confusion on Election Day, resulting in disenfranchisement of large numbers of voters, particularly with Blackwell's edicts restricting provisional balloting. In many cases, the eliminations were not accurately publicized. Since more voters were now coming to fewer precincts, these eliminations also resulted in more delays at primarily African-American and Democratic precincts, causing still more disenfranchisement.

Of Ohio's 88 counties, 20 suffered a significant reduction — shutting at least 20 percent (or at least 30) of their precincts. Those 20 counties went heavily to Gore in 2000, 53 to 42 percent. The other 68 counties, which underwent little-to-no precinct consolidation, went exactly the opposite way in 2000: 53 to 42 percent to Bush.

In the 68 counties that kept their precinct count at or near 2000 levels, Kerry benefited more than Bush from the high turnout, getting 24 percent more votes than Gore did in 2000, while Bush increased his vote total by only 17 percent.

But in the 20 squeezed counties, the opposite happened. Bush increased his vote total by 22 percent, and Kerry won just 19 percent more than Gore in 2000.

NOTES:

David S. Bernstein, "Questioning Ohio," the *Providence Phoenix*. See:
http://www.providencephoenix.com/features/other_stories/multi_1/documents/04259694.asp

26. Many registration books at polling stations were out-of-date, resulting in disenfranchisement.

According to sworn testimony given after the election, many of the polling books at the voting stations were out-of-date. Many long-time registered voters who had voted for decades at the same polling station found themselves unable to vote, and were also denied provisional ballots.

It is unclear how many voters were thus disenfranchised.

NOTES:

CICJ Hearings Testimony, op. cit.

Conyers Report, op. cit.

Conyers Testimony, op. cit.

Ney Testimony, op. cit.

DNC Report, op. cit.

Transcripts, "Fight Back with Fitrakis," WVKO-AM, November 2004 - August 2005.

Ray Beckerman, "Basic Report from Columbus," Freepress.org, November 5, 2004. This article appears in *Essential Documents*, p. 17.

27. Blackwell refused at least one request to have paper ballots available at polling stations to alleviate anticipated bottlenecks should there prove to be too few working voting machines (as did happen).

Prior to the election, William "Bill" Anthony, chair of the Franklin County Democratic Party and chair of the Franklin County Board of Elections, said he called Kenneth Blackwell on behalf of the Board. Anthony told the Secretary of State that the Franklin County Board was concerned that the large turnout expected on Election Day might overwhelm the available voting machines.

In order to eliminate the possibility of excessive waits on the part of prospective voters, Anthony asked Blackwell for permission to have paper ballots available. Their presence, said Anthony, would serve as a safety valve for machine shortages and malfunctions, and might save voters hours of waiting.

Blackwell refused the request. Anthony and the BOE did not aggressively or publicly pursue the issue.

NOTES:

Bill Anthony, with Bob Fitrakis, on "Fight Back with Fitrakis," WVKO-AM, November 2004.

Bill Anthony, with Harvey Wasserman, on "Fred Andrle Show," WOSU-AM, November 2004.

28. The Franklin County Board of Elections estimated it would need 5,000 machines for the November 2nd vote, but had only 2,866 available on Election Day.

Director Damschroder, BOE Chair Anthony and others confirmed before the election that Franklin County would need five thousand voting machines to handle the turnout expected on November 2nd. Only 2,866 were made available. In virtually all cases, the precincts shorted were in the heavily Democratic inner-city, resulting in substantial disenfranchisement.

NOTES:

Conyers Report, op. cit.

Ney Testimony, op. cit.

DNC Report, op. cit.

Widespread news reports in *The New York Times, Columbus Dispatch, Toledo Blade, Cleveland Plain Dealer.*

Anthony, "Fight Back," op. cit.

Anthony, "Andrle," op. cit.

Bob Fitrakis, "Document Reveals Columbus Voters Waited Hours as Election Officials Held Back Machines," Freepress.org, 11/16/04. This article is in *Essential Documents*, p. 35.

Franklin County Board of Elections Voting Machine Distribution Spreadsheet, *Essential Documents* pp. 22-26.

29. Seventy-six wards in Franklin County had fewer voting machines than in the primary election the previous spring.

In Franklin County, 76 wards had fewer voting machines available on November 2nd than they had during the spring primary election. All 76 wards were in the city of Columbus, rather than in the suburbs; 42 of the short-changed precincts were in predominantly African-American districts.

NOTES:

CICJ Hearings Testimony, op. cit.

Conyers Report, op. cit.

Conyers Testimony, op. cit.

Ney Testimony, op. cit.

DNC Report, op. cit.

Widespread news reports in *The New York Times, Columbus Dispatch, Toledo Blade, Cleveland Plain-Dealer.*

Anthony, "Fight Back," op. cit.

Anthony, "Andrle," op. cit.

Bob Fitrakis, "Document Reveals Columbus Voters Waited Hours as Election Officials Held Back Machines," Freepress.org, November 16, 2004. This article is in *Essential Documents,* p. 35.

Franklin County Board of Elections Voting Machine Distribution Spreadsheet
Essential Documents pp. 22-26.

30. Statewide shortages and misallocation of voting machines and other impediments led to long delays, that, when combined with an atmosphere of intimidation and other problems, may have prompted three (3) percent of the state's electorate to be disenfranchised, representing a vote total well in excess of Bush's official margin of victory.

According to sworn testimony given after the election, as well as expert statistical analysis, many tens of thousands of citizens who came to vote left without doing so because of the long delays. Many potential voters testified under oath that they returned to their polling stations two or three times in the hope that the lines had shortened.

In all reported instances, lines in fact stayed long right through the scheduled closing times of the impeded precincts. At closing time, some precinct workers then wrongfully dismissed citizens waiting to vote, adding thousands to the roles of those disenfranchised by the administrative errors of the election and the mal-distribution of the voting machines.

According to a study commissioned by the Democratic Party, as many as three (3) percent of the state's potential voters did not vote as a result of the long lines. Those interviewed who left the polls said they had to do so because of demands of work or child care.

With more than 5.6 million votes cast in Ohio, this would mean some 170,000 citizens failed to cast ballots they otherwise would have cast, far exceeding Bush's official 118,775 margin.

NOTES:

Beckerman, op. cit.

DNC Report, op. cit.

J.K. Galbraith, "Waiting to Vote," Salon.com, November 3. 2004. This article appears in *Essential Documents,* p. 20.

Mark Niquette, "G.O.P. Stronghold Saw Increase in Voting Machines," *Columbus Dispatch,* December 12, 2004.

31. African-American voters on average suffered far longer voting delays than white voters, indicating that the vast majority of Ohioans who failed to cast ballots due to long lines, intimidation, etc., would have cast them for Democratic candidates.

By all anecdotal accounts, and those given under oath after the election, voters who failed to cast votes due to the long delays were registered in inner-city, predominantly African-American precincts, which overall went more than 83% for Kerry. According to many or all who testified, those lines might have been avoided had Blackwell agreed to make paper ballots available, or had voting machines been properly provided and allocated, or had partisan challengers not been given access to the polling stations, further worsening delays in select precincts.

The belief that it was primarily African-Americans who were disenfranchised by the long delays was confirmed by a study commissioned by the Democratic Party that indicated that, statewide, African-Americans waited an average of nearly an hour to vote, while white voters waited an average of about ten minutes. In Franklin County, the wait in African-American wards was an average of three hours and fifteen minutes.

The Democratic study inexplicably asserted that those who failed to vote due to the delays may have been divided equally along party lines. But the Congressional Report commissioned by Rep. John Conyers strongly disagrees and characterizes the factors that resulted in the delays as part of a larger "Jim Crow" strategy to discourage blacks from voting.

Indeed, all credible evidence points unavoidably to the fact that it was primarily African-Americans who were disenfranchised and that the overt discrimination and sheer numbers involved might alone have been sufficient to shift the outcome of the presidential election.

NOTES:

CICJ Hearings Testimony, op. cit.

Conyers Report, op. cit.

Conyers Testimony, op. cit.

Ney Testimony, op. cit.

DNC Report, op. cit.

33. On absentee ballots, widespread reports indicate problems that may have been inflicted in a partisan way.

Amidst widespread complaints in the lead-up to the election, and in sworn testimony after the election, there appear to have been serious problems with absentee ballots that may have been inflicted in a partisan manner.

In Franklin County, co-author Harvey Wasserman applied in person for an absentee ballot, registering as a Democrat at the address where he has lived for twenty years. His precinct has also not moved.

Three days later, Wasserman received in the mail a notice that his application had an improper address. But the notice came to the proper address.

His wife, registered as an independent at the same address, had no such problems.

When he called the election board to complain, the worker there told Wasserman that the board was receiving "hundreds" of similar calls from voters complaining about rejections of applications for absentee ballots.

After four phone calls, Wasserman did receive an absentee ballot. In sworn testimony taken after the election, numerous other registered voters testified to similar experiences. In at least one case, a voter finally received an absentee ballot on election eve and then personally drove several hours to the home polling station to cast it.

In sworn testimony taken after the election, similar experiences were reported from all over the state. (There were also widespread problems involving at least 56,000 absentee ballots in Florida, as discussed in part later in this book).

NOTES:

CICJ Hearings Testimony, op. cit.

Conyers Report, op. cit.

Conyers Testimony, op. cit.

Ney Testimony, op. cit.

DNC Report, op. cit.

Franklin County Board of Elections, Letter to Harvey Wasserman, September 14, 2004. This letter appears in *Essential Documents*, p. 37.

34. Provisional ballots were denied to voters who never received their absentee ballots.

Sworn testimony taken after the election indicates that some voters who never received their absentee ballots and then took the trouble to get themselves physically to their polling stations on Election Day were denied the right to cast provisional ballots because they were told they should have received an absentee ballot. Reports from Cuyahoga and other counties indicate hundreds of voters never got their absentee ballots in the mail.

NOTES:

Conyers Report, op. cit.

Conyers Testimony, op. cit.

CICJ Hearings Transcripts, op. cit.

35. Absentee ballots were delivered pre-punched for George W. Bush.

Sworn testimony taken after the election indicates a number of voters received absentee ballots that were pre-punched for George W. Bush. Given the way the ballots were tallied, an attempt to vote for a presidential candidate other than George W. Bush on such a ballot would result in an overvote that would not be counted for president.

Discovering that absentee ballots had been pre-punched was not a given. In some cases the ballots came in the form of punch cards housed in envelopes. The voter was then to punch through the envelope. But if the punch card inside had been pre-punched without the envelope also having been pre-punched, the voter would not know. The ballot would then have two punches for president, making it an "overvote" that would then be discarded.

NOTES:

Conyers Report, op. cit.

Conyers Testimony, op. cit.

CICJ Hearings Transcripts, op. cit.

36. Absentee ballots were distributed that were impossible to understand, or were deliberately misleading.

In forms reminiscent of the butterfly ballots that caused chaos in Florida 2000, absentee ballots were mailed to Ohio voters in various counties that were virtually impossible to understand or were deliberately misleading.

On some absentee forms, John Kerry's name appeared third on the list of candidates, but the voter was required to punch hole 4 to vote for him. Punching hole 3 resulted in a vote for George W. Bush.

NOTES:

Testimony of James Hansen in *CICJ Transcripts,* op. cit.

37. In Hamilton County, some absentee ballots were mailed that did not contain an option to vote for John Kerry and John Edwards.

Sworn testimony taken after the election, confirmed by the National Voting Rights Institute, asserted that a number of absentee ballots were mailed in Hamilton County that did not provide the ability to vote for the Kerry-Edwards ticket.

NOTES:

"Kerry's Name Omitted from Some Ballots," *Columbus Dispatch,* October 19, 2003.

Moss v. Bush, op. cit. This incident is listed as #107.

38. The Republican Party sent threatening letters to students likely to vote absentee, challenging their right to do so.

Sworn testimony indicates that the Republican Party sent pre-election mailings to thousands of students in Franklin and other Ohio counties challenging their right to vote absentee.

In Franklin County, the unprecedented mass mailing was followed by an announcement from Republican Board of Elections Director Damschroder that the county would rent a large hall on the Thursday before Election Day. The announcement indicated that all students who were Franklin County residents but who were studying out of town and who intended to vote absentee would have to be present to face these GOP challenges. A judge halted the mass challenge, but the GOP never withdrew the threat.

NOTES:

Fitrakis & Wasserman, "Twelve Ways....," op. cit.

Conyers Report, op. cit.

39. The Cincinnati Board of Elections removed 105,000 registered voters from its rolls prior to Election Day.

In the four years leading up to the 2004 contest, the Hamilton County (Cincinnati) Board of Elections removed some 105,000 registered voters, on the pretext that they had not voted in the last two federal elections.

The purge was conducted by the Board's Director, a Republican. The move was unprecedented, but is now being duplicated by the Republican Director of the Franklin County Board of Elections.

NOTES:

Fitrakis & Wasserman, "Twelve Ways....," op. cit.

Hamilton County Board of Election Registration Data.

40. Extra-legal threats to some 34,000 ex-felons, and to additional individuals who were indicted on felonies but were never convicted, were issued by Boards of Elections in twenty Republican-dominated counties.

Officials in twenty GOP-dominated counties issued letters to some 34,000 former felons challenging their right to vote. In Hamilton County, officials falsely told former felons they needed written permission from a judge to cast a vote.

The ban on voting by ex-felons originated with the eleven former states of the Confederacy. It was initiated by white racists after the Civil War to help prevent freed blacks from voting. Today, ex-felons generally vote heavily Democratic.

In Ohio, ex-felons do have the right to vote unless they are currently incarcerated. That right extends to ex-felons who are on probation or in halfway houses. But the letters from the twenty counties created an atmosphere of intimidation and confusion among those ex-felons contemplating whether or not to vote.

NOTES:

Matt Damschroder, Interview with Bob Fitrakis, "Fight Back With Fitrakis," WVKO-AM Radio, November, 2004.

Prison Reform Advocacy Center, "The Disenfranchisement of the Re-Enfranchised," cited in *Essential Documents*, p. 9.

Bob Fitrakis, "Presidential Election at Risk: Ohio's Electoral System Riddled with Flaws," FreePress.org, September 20, 2004.

Fitrakis & Wasserman, "Twelve Ways....," op. cit.

41. In 2004 Franklin County alone sent 3,500 letters of cancellation to ex-felons, and to individuals indicted on felonies but not convicted, more than ten times the normal number.

Board of Elections Director Matt Damschroder has admitted that Franklin County, which each year normally cancels the voting rights of 2-300 convicted felons, this year sent 3,500 letters of cancellation to both felons and ex-felons whose convictions date back to 1998. With few exceptions, the ex-felons were actually eligible to vote and should not have been told otherwise. According to Damschroder, the order to send such a large number of letters came from Blackwell.

NOTES:

Matt Damschroder, "Interview" with Bob Fitrakis, "Fight Back With Fitrakis," WVKO-AM Radio, November, 2004.

Prison Reform Advocacy Center, "The Disenfranchisement of the Re-Enfranchised," cited in *Essential Documents*, p. 9.

Fitrakis, "Presidential Election at Risk," op. cit.

Fitrakis & Wasserman, "Twelve Ways....," op. cit.

42. The threats to ex-felons issued in Franklin County extended to citizens who were not ex-felons.

Under Damschroder's direction, and allegedly under orders from Blackwell, the list of 3500 cancellation letters issued to current and ex-felons, informing them they did not have the right to vote, included numerous citizens who had been charged with felonies but were convicted only of misdemeanors. For them, an additional and entirely extra-legal hurdle against voting had been created.

As mentioned, Damschroder later told WVKO Radio, on the "Fitrakis Files" program, that he normally sends 2-300 such letters in an election year, but that in 2004 he sent 3500 under orders from Secretary of State Blackwell. This letter may well have discouraged many citizens who were never convicted of any felony from voting.

How many Ohio citizens were thus disenfranchised is unclear.

NOTES:

Matt Damschroder, "Interview" with Bob Fitrakis, "Fight Back With Fitrakis," WVKO-AM Radio, November, 2004.

Prison Reform Advocacy Center, "The Disenfranchisement of the Re-Enfranchised," cited in *Essential Documents*, p. 9.

Bob Fitrakis, "Presidential Election at Risk," op. cit.

Fitrakis & Wasserman, "Twelve Ways....," op. cit.

Mark A. Wofford, Interview with Bob Fitrakis. Wofford was a student at Columbus State Community College who voted as a registered Republican for many years. When he switched party affiliation he received a letter from the BOE telling him he could not vote because he was an ex-felon. He had been charged with a felony in 1998, but was never convicted. Thus he was not an ex-felon. Under Ohio law, ex-felons have the right to vote anyway.

43. A GOP activist "Mighty Texas Strike Force" targeted ex-felons with threatening phone calls aimed at intimidating them from voting.

Eye witnesses indicate a "Mighty Texas Strike Force" camped at Columbus's downtown Holiday Inn and made calls from pay phones to what was apparently a list of ex-felons, threatening that, if they tried to vote on Election Day, they would be re-arrested.

It is not clear where the GOP group got the list of alleged ex-felons. Their actions were likely illegal under the Voting Rights Act of 1965. Their presence in Columbus was widely reported, and it was well-known what they were doing. But they were never prosecuted, despite a 911 call in Columbus.

Voters have testified in other Ohio cities that they were threatened on the phone and at the polling stations with arrest for back child support and parking tickets, the latter a non-felony.

NOTES:

Nick Mottern, "The Mighty Texas Strike Force," Documentary News Service, February 28, 2005. This article appears in *Essential Documents*, p. 159.

Fitrakis Statement, *Conyers Report*, op. cit.

44. Dis-informational fliers threatening attacks against civil rights and voter registration groups and those who registered with them were widely circulated in inner-city precincts.

A series of threatening fliers, some of which were printed on what appeared to be official letterhead from county election boards, were circulated through inner city precincts with deliberate misinformation about the voter registration process.

In particular, some fliers warned that citizens who had been registered by the National Association for the Advancement of Colored People (NAACP), America Coming Together (ACT), or the Kerry Campaign had in fact not been properly registered. Some of the fliers implied that citizens registered by such groups might be involved in an illegality.

Similar fliers were circulated in other states.

NOTES:

"Lake County Board of Elections," "Urgent Advisory," circulated anonymously, October 22, 2004. This flier is reproduced in *Essential Documents*, p. 19. Its true authorship is unclear.

Conyers Report, op. cit.

DNC Report, op. cit.

Transcript, "Fight Back with Fitrakis," WVKO-AM, 10/04-8/05.

45. Fliers with misleading information about times and places for voting were widely circulated in inner-city precincts around the state.

A wide range of fliers, many of them also on what appeared to be official letterhead, told inner- city voters that, due to an expected heavy turnout, Tuesday, November 2nd, was the day for Republicans to vote. Wednesday, November 3rd, would be for Democrats. The fliers also often gave wrong information about where people were to vote.

NOTES:

"Lake County Board of Elections," "Urgent Advisory," op. cit.

Conyers Report, op. cit.

DNC Report, op. cit.

Transcript, "Fight Back with Fitrakis," WVKO-AM, October 04 - August 05.

46. Phone calls with deliberately misleading information were made to potential Ohio voters by parties purporting to represent local election boards.

The *Columbus Dispatch* (which endorsed George W. Bush for president) and WVKO Radio both documented phone calls being made by people impersonating official election workers directing registered voters to incorrect polling sites. One individual was falsely instructed not to vote at the polling station across the street from his house but to go to a "new" polling station four miles away. Under Blackwell's rules, the misdirected voter would not have been given a provisional ballot.

NOTES:

"Lake County Board of Elections," "Urgent Advisory," circulated anonymously, October 22, 2004. This flier is reproduced in *Essential Documents*, p. 19. Its true authorship is unclear.

Conyers Report, op. cit.

DNC Report, op. cit.

Transcripts, "Fight Back with Fitrakis," WVKO-AM, October, 2004 to August, 2005.

47. According to U.S. Senate Minority Leader Harry Reid, misleading fliers similar to those distributed in Ohio were also distributed in Nevada.

In a meeting after the election with Rev. Jesse Jackson, co-author Bob Fitrakis and others, U.S. Senator Harry Reid confirmed that fliers were widely distributed in Las Vegas and elsewhere in Nevada spreading misinformation about voting dates, places and registration requirements. Similar fliers are known to have been distributed in North Carolina and Georgia.

How many American citizens were thus disenfranchised is unclear.

NOTES:

U.S. Senator Harry Reid, in a meeting with Rev. Jesse Jackson, Bob Fitrakis, et. al., Washington DC, 1/5/05.

48. In Orlando, Florida, widespread police action targeted African-American election organizers, including key members of voter registration teams and the mayor.

Prior to the 2004 election, state troopers conducted a sweeping "investigation" that targeted organizers of a highly successful voter registration drive that focussed on the African-American community. Indictments were issued on trumped-up charges that outraged civil libertarians and the civil rights community throughout the United States. Among others, Mayor Buddy Dyer, a popular Democrat, was suspended from office.

After the election, all charges were dropped. But the harassment, which marred a campaign in which Gov. Jeb Bush was seeking re-election, was universally acknowledged to have had a chilling effect on the attempt to bring African-Americans to the Florida polls.

NOTES:

Bob Herbert, "Suppress the Vote," *New York Times*, Editorial page, August 6, 2004.

Bob Herbert, "Voting While Black," *New York Times*, Editorial page, August 20, 2004.

Bob Herbert, "A Chill in Florida," *New York Times*, Editorial page, August 23, 2004.

Bob Herbert, "Voting Without All the Facts," *New York Times*, Editorial page, November 8, 2004.

49. In Broward County, Florida, some 56,000 absentee ballots were "mistakenly" left without being sent.

As in Franklin County and elsewhere in Ohio, Broward County, Florida, reported serious problems with absentee ballots. Broward BOE election officials failed to mail some 56,000 absentee ballots in time for the election.

NOTES:

Medea Benjamin & Deborah James, "Florida's Palm Beach County Bracing for the Electoral Storm," Truthout.org, November 2, 2004.

50. In Broward and West Palm Beach Counties, Florida, 8,000 absentee ballots were given to the U.S. Postal Service just three days before the election.

The U.S. Postal Service complained that Board of Elections officials from Broward and West Palm Beach Counties, Florida, showed up at post offices with some 8,000 absentee ballots just three days before Election Day, casting serious doubt as to whether they would be received in time to have the votes cast and counted properly.

NOTES:

Benjamin & Jones, "Florida's Palm Beach...," op. cit.

PR Newswire, October 31, 2004.

51. Broward County, Florida, acknowledged that 51,000 absentee ballots were returned out of some 127,000 emailed out. The Broward BOE apparently decided to send out a second batch.

News reports in south Florida indicated that more than 51,000 absentee ballots mailed out by the Broward County Board of Elections came back in the mail. The Broward BOE decided to re-mail them on October 28, less than a week prior to Election Day.

NOTES:

http://www.NBC6.net/news/3867358/detail.html

Chapter Two:

Election Day:
November 2, 2004

1. On Election Day, George W. Bush may have met with Secretary of State Blackwell and Franklin County Board of Elections Director Damschroder.

On Election Day, co-author Bob Fitrakis was told, in front of witnesses, at the Board of Elections, that President Bush was meeting with Secretary Blackwell and Director Damschroder. Fitrakis was working as an election monitor in Columbus and went to the BOE office to complain to Damschroder about the shortage of voting machines in inner-city precincts.

When Fitrakis asked to talk with Damschroder, BOE staff told him the Director was meeting with the President and the Secretary of State. Bush made several public campaign appearances in Columbus that day.

Election protection activists had hoped to ask Damschroder, Blackwell and Bush about this possible meeting, but they all refused to appear under oath despite notices at depositions.

NOTES:

Bob Fitrakis, meeting with election officials, Franklin County Board of Elections, Columbus, Ohio, November 2, 2004.

Columbus *Dispatch*, "Judge orders officials to provide paper ballots," November 2, 2004, www.dispatch.com.

"J. Kenneth Blackwell's Notice of Deposition, Scheduled for Monday, December 7, 2004," in *Essential Documents,* Legal Documents section.

2. Misallocation of voting machines resulted in extremely long lines in inner-city precincts of Columbus and other Ohio urban centers, areas that were disproportionately African-American.

Record turnouts throughout Ohio 2004, which had been widely predicted, resulted in stresses on many voting stations. But nowhere were the lines longer on the whole than in the overwhelmingly Democratic African-American wards in Columbus.

As per Ohio law, the Franklin County Board of Elections is bi-partisan. But its Director, Matt Damschroder, is a conservative Republican. On Election Day, 2004, Damschroder oversaw a mal-distribution of voting machines that resulted in huge lines at inner-city voting stations. (Project Censored voted the Freepress.org coverage of this story as one of the Most Censored Stories of 2004.)

According to sworn testimony, innumerable eyewitness reports and video, tens of thousands of inner-city residents waited three hours or more to cast their ballots. Additional thousands left and came back two and three times, hoping the lines would diminish, which they did not. Others testified to staying away altogether once news spread about the length of the wait to vote. The longest wait in Franklin County was seven hours.

The lines were caused by strategic shortages of voting machines. Commonly accepted estimates prior to the election indicated Franklin County would need about 5,000 voting machines to handle the expected November 2. Despite that clear warning, Damschroder delivered just 2,741 machines to Franklin County polling places on election morning.

Throughout the day, inner-city poll workers made desperate calls to the Board of Election headquarters, pleading for more machines. Some were delivered late in the day. At least 76 were held back until the polls were near closing. At least 68 were never delivered at all.

Statewide, as many as 2,000 machines may have been left in storage by various election officials. These machines were never delivered to polling places despite long lines which developed not only in Columbus, but in Cleveland, Cincinnati, Toledo and elsewhere.

As mentioned earlier, prior to the election, Secretary of State Blackwell also rejected a request to allow paper ballots to be available in precincts where a shortage of voting machines was expected. The availability of such ballots almost certainly would have reduced the waiting time for inner-city voters, and thus would have raised the numbers of citizens who did cast a ballot.

Co-author Bob Fitrakis, legal advisor for the Election Protection Coalition, lodged a formal protest at the Franklin County BOE, requesting more voting machines for his precinct. He was told by Democratic BOE member Marlene Wirth: "It's people like you that are the problem." It was then Fitrakis was told by a security officer that Damschroder was meeting with President Bush and Secretary of State Blackwell.

NOTES:

Bob Fitrakis and Harvey Wasserman, "How a Republican Supervisor Manipulated the Vote in Black and White: Freepress.org, November 23, 2004. This appears in *Essential Documents*, p. 48

CICJ Hearings Testimony, op. cit.

Conyers Report, op. cit.

Conyers Testimony, op. cit.

Ney Testimony, op. cit.

DNC Report, op cit.

The assertion that the state had an extra 2,000 voting machines in storage that were not deployed to help people vote on November 2 was told to Bob Fitrakis by a government employee on condition of anonymity in an unpublished interview, November, 2004.

Niquette, "G.O.P. Stronghold Saw...," op. cit.

3. At the Linden Library and elsewhere in the inner-city dual precincts in Franklin County, lines were separate and unmarked, causing many voters to wait in the wrong line, resulting in very long waits, confusion and disenfranchisement.

At the Linden Library in Franklin County, voters were forced to wait through one line to sign in and get a voter slip, then to wait in another one to vote. The lines were not marked and voters often waited through the wrong line, causing extreme delays.

Lines in other dual precincts were also not marked, causing numerous prospective voters to leave or to cast provisional ballots, many of which were never counted.

NOTES:

CICJ Hearings Transcripts, op. cit.

4. The distribution of voting machines in Franklin County was demographically selective.

Franklin County has long been a Republican bastion. But in recent years the city of Columbus has become Democratic. In 1999, Democrat Michael Coleman was elected as the city's first African-American mayor. All seven members of Columbus City Council are Democrats.

On Election Day, 2004, voters in precincts in the predominantly Republican suburbs surrounding Columbus experienced virtually no waiting time. There were no reported shortages of machines. The World Harvest Church, home of Rev. Rod Parsley, a prominent fundamentalist supporter of George W. Bush and Kenneth Blackwell, had a surplus of voting machines. Other Republican enclaves such as Canal Winchester, Dublin and Walden O'Dell's Upper Arlington reported no waits for voting, in many cases receiving more voting machines in 2004 than in 2000.

But in the overwhelmingly African-American inner-city wards, where Democrats received more than 80% of the vote, the shortages were critical. Despite desperate phone calls from frustrated poll workers, the shortages lasted throughout the day and into the evening.

On Election Day, Damschroder lied under oath about various aspects of the distribution process. Among other things, Damschroder claimed there was no mal-distribution of machines at all. The Congressional Report commissioned by Rep. Conyers charged that the selective supply of machines was motivated both by race and by the desire of Republican officials to minimize the Democratic turnout, which they clearly succeeded in doing.

NOTES:

CICJ Hearings Transcripts, op. cit.

Michael Powell & Peter Slevin, "Several Factors Contributed to 'Lost' Voters in Ohio," *Washington Post*, December 15, 2004. This article cites the possible loss of 15,000 to 20,000 votes due to long delays at polling stations in central Ohio.

Matt Damschroder, testimony in Federal Court for the Southern District of Ohio Northern Division, Columbus, Ohio, November 2, 2004.

Conyers Report, op. cit.

Niquette, "G.O.P. Stronghold saw...," op. cit.

DNC Report, op. cit.

5. GOP challengers were illegally allowed into off-limits areas in at least one central Ohio precinct.

Sworn testimony confirmed after the election that in one heavily Republican ward in the wealthiest precinct in the Franklin County suburb of Bexley, at least one Republican challenger was given extraordinary access. According to the eyewitness, the GOP challenger was allowed to sit at the registration table, which is illegal.

The challenger apparently relinquished the position only after being confronted three times. However, precinct election officials were reported as being extremely hostile to the voter requesting that the GOP challenger abide by the law.

The number of other precincts in which this behavior was repeated is unclear.

NOTES:

CICJ Hearings Transcripts, op. cit. Testimony that the Bexley precinct allowed a GOP challenger into restricted areas came from Tom Kessel. His testimony appears in "Essential Documents," p. 59.

Fitrakis & Wasserman, "New Ohio Voter Transcripts Feed Floodtide of Doubt About Republican Election Manipulation," Freepress.org, November 25, 2004.

6. Republican challengers did play a significant role in delaying the vote and intimidating voters in inner-city precincts.

Sworn testimony after the election confirmed that, in many inner-city precincts, Republican challengers working close to registration tables did intimidate would-be voters, in some instances prompting them to leave without voting.

As had been rumored before the election, the challengers also served to confuse the voting process and to lengthen already very long waits for inner-city residents hoping to vote. The *Conyers Report* referred to these incidents as part of a larger Republican "Jim Crow" strategy to drive down the African-American vote.

NOTES:

CICJ Hearings Transcripts, op. cit.

Mark Niquette, "Finally, It's Time to Vote," *Columbus Dispatch*, November 2, 2004, p. 1A.

"Voters Challenged; Given Provisional Ballots; Provisionals Not Handled Properly," in *Essential Documents*, p. 67.

Conyers Report, op. cit.

7. Partisan police officers joined with Republican challengers to threaten Democratic voters.

In a sworn statement after the election, an election observer reported that in twelve polls in Westlake, Republican officials joined with police offers and GOP election judges to threaten and intimidate Democratic voters, "removing legally posted Democratic messages, and chasing Democratic supporters from the polling places with the threat of arrest."

A number of witnesses testified to polling stations being swarmed with police cars whose officers were often hostile. According to one witness, when police were confronted over their intimidation tactics, one responded: "If they are intimidated, then they shouldn't vote."

While threatening Democratic poll workers, Republican election judges harshly challenged potential Democratic voters, driving many away from the polls.

NOTES:

Dr. Werner Lange, "Kerry Votes Switched to Bush and Ballots Pre-Punched for Bush," Freepress.org, December 24, 2004.

8. Cars legally parked by voters at inner-city precincts were towed while they were voting or waiting in line.

Sworn testimony after the election confirms that inner-city voting access was also disrupted by GOP officials who ordered cars towed while voters waited in line. Numerous central city precincts had too few parking spaces to accommodate the large turnout. In some instances, even cars that were legally parked were towed while their owners waited in line to vote. At the Driving Park precinct in Columbus, city trucks attempted to block off areas that were otherwise legal for parking.

NOTES:

CICJ Hearings Transcripts, op. cit.

9. At least one Republican property owner asked prospective voters, many African-American, to leave a polling station before they could vote.

Sworn testimony given after the election confirms that a prominent Republican activist, whose funeral home was being used as a polling station, demanded that inner-city voters leave the premises before they had voted.

NOTES:

CICJ Hearings Transcripts, op. cit. Michael Hayes testified on November 13, 2004 that a "well-known Republican business-man in the community" was telling prospective voters to "please disperse, please get into your cars." In *Essential Documents*, op. cit.

10. In inner-city precincts, prospective voters who were in line at the polling stations' 7:30 closing time were illegally sent away without being allowed to vote.

Ohio election law states that anyone in line waiting to vote at the precinct's closing time is entitled access to a polling station to cast a ballot, even if it has to be done after closing time. This statute was enforced by a court-ordered Temporary Restraining Order in Knox County and Franklin County.

But at inner-city precincts in Columbus, film crews documented registered voters waiting in line to vote who were sent away at precisely 7:30. In at least one case, the polling station's door was locked and prospective voters who had waited outside in the rain for hours were summarily dismissed without being allowed to vote.

NOTES:

CICJ Hearings Testimony, op. cit.

Conyers Report, op. cit.

Conyers Testimony, op. cit.

Linda Byrket, "Video the Vote," November 2, 2004.

11. In Knox County, students at Kenyon College and citizens of Gambier waited up to eleven hours to vote, while there was no wait at a nearby fundamentalist college.

In sworn testimony taken after the election, and as presented in a wide range of media reports, students at Kenyon College and citizens of the town of Gambier were forced to wait up to eleven hours to vote. The precinct went heavily for Kerry. Though warned of a likely large turnout, election officials had only two voting machines present to handle the influx. One of them broke down early in the morning, resulting in what may have been the longest lines in the state.

By 7:30 pm, at the scheduled closing of the polling station, hundreds of students had yet to vote. A court order kept the voting station open, with the last students casting their ballots around 4 am.

At the nearby fundamentalist Mt. Vernon Nazarene University, there were ample voting machines, and no waiting at any time through the day. Voters there went heavily for George W. Bush.

NOTES:

Christopher Hitchens, "Ohio's Odd Numbers," *Vanity Fair,* March, 2005.

CICJ Hearings Testimony, op. cit.

Conyers Report, op. cit.

Conyers Testimony, op. cit.

DNC Report, op. cit.

12. Students at Oberlin College and residents of the town of Oberlin experienced waits similar to those at Kenyon College and Gambier.

Students at Oberlin College, in northern Ohio, and residents of the town of Oberlin, also suffered waits of up to six hours.

Founded in 1833, Oberlin was America's first co-educational college. Voters from the town and school went heavily for John Kerry.

NOTES:

Free Press Transcripts, op. cit. This incident appears in *Essential Documents,* p. 62.

13. At Wilberforce College, mostly African-American students were illegally challenged during the registration process.

Sworn testimony taken after the election confirmed that at Wilberforce College in Wilmington, African-American students were illegally forced to provide photo ID in order to obtain a ballot. The process resulted in significant delays. As a result, many students apparently opted not to vote.

NOTES:

Conyers Report, op. cit.

Conyers Testimony, op. cit.

14. In Lucas County, malfunctioning machines caused very long lines and disenfranchisement of inner-city residents.

In heavily Democratic inner city wards of Lucas County (Toledo), voting machines broke down early in the day. Some were never fixed. Huge lines ensued. As in Franklin County, many citizens turned away and never voted.

Lucas County Election Director Paula Hicks-Hudson confirmed that Diebold opti-scan machines, which were being used instead of the Sequoia machines brought in by former BOE chair Tom Noe, had jammed in tests the week before the election, and were not fixed by Election Day.

NOTES:

CICJ Hearings Testimony, op. cit.

Conyers Report, op. cit.

Conyers Testimony, op. cit.

DNC Report, op. cit.

See also general coverage in the *Toledo Blade*.

15. In one Lucas County precinct, voting machines were completely inaccessible at the start of the day, with many citizens being disenfranchised.

At Glenwood Elementary School in Lucas County, voters in this largely African-American precinct expected to cast their ballots at 7 am.

However, the voting machines had been locked in the office of the principal. When the principal called in sick, the citizens who came to vote that morning were effectively disenfranchised.

NOTES:

CICJ Hearings Transcripts, op. cit.

16. In Lucas County, ballot markers were distributed that would not work on ballots, disenfranchising those who used them.

Sworn testimony indicates that someone in Lucas County provided voters with markers that would not work on ballots being cast, thus disenfranchising anyone who used them without their knowing it.

NOTES:

CICJ Hearings Transcripts, Lucas County. Chaired by Robert J. Fitrakis, Esq.

17. In Mahoning County (Youngstown) voting machines were recalibrated in the middle of Election Day, creating long lines and casting doubt on the vote count.

In Mahoning County (Youngstown), between twenty and thirty ES&S iVotronic machines broke down in the middle of the voting process and had to be recalibrated because voters were complaining that they tried to vote for one candidate but the machine indicated that a vote for a different candidate was being recorded.

Long lines resulted, and the veracity of the vote count was put in doubt.

NOTES:

CICJ Hearings Transcripts, op. cit.

Fitrakis & Wasserman, "New Ohio Voter Transcripts Feed Floodtide of Doubt About Republican Election Manipulation," Freepress.org., November 25, 2005.

Conyers Report, op. cit.

18. The "vote hopping" from Kerry to Bush that led to voting machine shutdowns in Mahoning County was also noted in Franklin County.

In sworn testimony taken after the election, voters in Mahoning County reported pushing John Kerry's name on their touchscreen voting machines and having George W. Bush's name light up. In sworn testimony after the election, one voter said this "vote hopping" happened repeatedly on his machine, and that an election official confirmed that it had been doing that "all day." The poll worker suggested he keep pushing Kerry's name until it stuck.

Other Mahoning County voters complained that they touched Kerry's name on the screen and it lit up, but that the light had gone out by the time they finished the rest of the ballot and returned to the top. Similar complaints about disappearing Kerry votes were sworn to in Franklin County. Voters claimed that the Kerry vote faded away, recording no vote for president.

NOTES:

CICJ Hearings Testimony, op. cit. Testimony on this issue appears in Essential Documents, pp. 69-70.

19. The long lines in Franklin, Lucas, Mahoning, Hamilton and other Ohio Counties discriminated against the elderly and infirm, in violation of the requirements of HAVA.

Eyewitness accounts, and sworn testimony taken after the election confirms that many of those disenfranchised due to the long lines at voting stations in Franklin and other counties were the elderly and infirm. In a short period of time on Election Day, investigators from the Columbus Free Press observed a dozen such handicapped individuals leaving the polls rather than waiting to vote as a result of the lines.

The Help America Vote Act and the Americans with Disabilities Act contain provisions that make this illegal.

NOTES:

Conyers Report, op. cit. Testimony on this appears in Essential Documents, p. 332.

Bob Fitrakis, Testimony at "Ohio Election Irregularities Congressional Forum," Washington DC, December 8, 2004. This testimony is at Essential Documents, p. 97.

Powell & Slevin, "Several Factors Contributed to 'Lost' Voters in Ohio," Washington Post, op. cit.

20. Bilingual assistance was unavailable in largely Hispanic precincts, disenfranchising Spanish-speaking voters.

Sworn testimony given after the election indicates that large numbers of Hispanic voters were disenfranchised because there were no Spanish-speaking poll workers or printed Spanish language instructions in heavily Hispanic precincts.

At one heavily Hispanic polling station there were thirteen election workers, none of whom spoke Spanish. Spanish-speaking voters later complained that their names were misspelled on registration lists and their ballots were spoiled because they could not read the instructions.

Overall, when their votes were counted, Hispanic voters in Ohio went heavily Democratic.

NOTES:

CICJ Hearings Transcripts, op. cit.

Phillips Report, op. cit.

21. In 2004, under Chair Bernadette Noe, the Lucas County Board of Elections purged some 28,000 voters from the registration rolls, including some who had voted without changing residence for four decades.

In a January 9, 2005 article, the *Toledo Blade* reported that during the summer of 2004, 28,000 voters were "erased" from the Lucas County voter registration rolls. The purge included voters like Barbara and Ralph George "who first registered to vote for John F. Kennedy in 1960 and had lived in the same East Toledo house for 44 years." The Georges had called the Board of Elections prior to their elimination from the voting rolls and had been told that they were eligible voters.

NOTES:

Fritz Wenzel, "Purging of rolls, confusion angers voters" *Toledo Blade,* January 9, 2005.

22. Provisional ballots cast in Lucas County precinct 4N were almost all rejected, including many cast by voters who were in the right room but the wrong line on Election Day.

The *Blade* also reported that 40 of the 43 provisional voters—many of them African-American—in Lucas County precinct 4N who were in the right room but the wrong precinct line on Election Day, had their provisional ballots rejected. Overall 50 of the 67 provisional ballots cast in precinct 4N were rejected. The volume of provisional ballots more than doubled when contrasted to the 2000 presidential election.

NOTES:

Fritz Wenzel, "Purging of rolls...," op. cit.

Chapter Three:

Election Night and the Exit Polls

1. On Election Night, immediately after the polls closed, Warren County GOP officials inexplicably declared a Homeland Security alert and excluded all media observers from the vote count.

When the polls closed on Election Night, the Republican executives of Warren County's election board suddenly announced that a Homeland Security alert was in effect. All materials relating to the vote count were confiscated by GOP officials, who ordered media representatives out of the process, in contradiction to long-standing practice. They moved the ballots from an officially sanctioned site to an unsanctioned warehouse, raising suspicions.

Later investigations indicate that before Election Day, discussions had occurred in Warren County election circles about the possibility of a Homeland Security alert during the vote count. But no confirmation of any authorization of such an alert ever came from the FBI or any other federal agency that might have been authorized to call one.

Warren County officials have issued no documented explanation for the origin of the Homeland Security alert.

The Warren County official vote count ultimately went extraordinarily heavily for George W. Bush, giving him as many as 14,000 more votes than he got in 2000, accounting for a substantial share of his official margin of victory in Ohio. As will be discussed, numerous large-scale anomalies surfaced in the bitterly contested vote count there, casting serious doubt on the veracity of the outcome.

An employee of the Warren County Board of Elections supplied the *Free Press* with a hand-drawn map showing an unauthorized warehouse where she alleges ballots were diverted following the Homeland Security alert.

NOTES:

Eric Solvig, "Warren County Still Counting," Cincinnati Enquirer, November 3, 2004.

Eric Solvig, "Warren Co. Defends Lockdown Decision," Cincinnati Enquirer, November 10, 2004.

Conyers Report, op. cit. Section IA, "Warren County Lockdown."

Bob Fitrakis, "How Blackwell and Petro saved Bush's brain," map, pg. 15, Free Press, vol. 35, no. 2, May-June 2005.

Moss v. Bush, op. cit.

2. Worldwide, the science of exit polling has become the gold standard for evaluating the will of the electorate.

The question of the accuracy of exit polls versus "official" vote counts cuts to the core of the modern electoral process. In the broadening global circle surrounding the science of evaluating elections and the credibility of "elected" governments, exit polls have come to be considered a more reliable measure of an electorate's will than the actual vote count. At the very least, they are the "gold standard" for checking the accuracy of ballot tallies.

In recent years, a significant variation between exit polls and an actual vote count has become viewed as a serious indication that there is a problem with the vote count, not the polling data. Extremely advanced, well-funded, state-of-the art polling done by Edison/Mitofsky, Roper, Gallup, Harris, Zogby and other polling organizations has become a bellweather for the

response of the international community to the legitimacy of governments claiming electoral mandates.
The most recent instance of exit polls trumping what almost certainly was a rigged vote count came in Ukraine, just prior to America's 2004 election. There, international pressure joined with local protest to force what amounted to a nonviolent electoral revolution. Armed with exit polling data that confirmed their "anecdotal" evidence of massive fraud and vote theft in a presidential contest, the people of Ukraine overturned a national election, forced a new one, then threw out an incumbent who had claimed victory.

A similar uprising, again fueled in part by polling data, resulted in the resignation of Edouard Scheverdnaze from the presidency of the former Soviet republic of Georgia. In 1994, the PRI, Mexico's dominant party, turned to exit pollsters like Warren Mitofsky to monitor the country's 2000 election so that it might be certified as valid in the eyes of the world. Perhaps because of that, the PRI lost the presidency in 2000 for the first time in seventy years.

Along with other former Soviet republics and the Philippines, major American media have also invested heavily in exit polling. On election night 2004, the National Election Pool (NEP) was formed by the ABC, AP, CBS, NBC, CNN and Fox Networks to provide viewers with accurate, up-to-date assessments of who was winning the American election. Their chosen method was by exit polling, anchored by the Mitofsky organization.

NOTES:

Bob Fitrakis, "Unanswered Exit Poll Questions," ColumbusAlive.com, November 16, 2000. This appears in "Essential Documents," p. 217.

Steven F. Freeman, "The Unexplained Exit Poll Discrepancy," A Research Report from the University of Pennsylvania;, December 29, 2004. See stfreeman@sas.upenn.edu.

Jonathan D. Simon and Ron P. Baiman, "The 2004 Presidential Election: Who Won the Popular Vote? An Examination of the Comparative Validity of Exit Poll and Vote Count Data," Freepress.org, January 2, 2004.

Steven F. Freeman, "Stolen or Lost," AlterNet, January 20, 2005.

Steven F. Freeman & Josh Mitteldorf, "A Corrupted Election: Despite What You May Have Heard, the Exit Polls Were Right," *In These Times,* February 15, 2005.

Ron Baiman, Affidavit, *Moss v. Bush,* op. cit.

---

3. *On Election Night, 2004, America's exit polls showed a nationwide victory for John Kerry of about 1.5 million votes.*

On Election Night 2004, up until about 12:30 am on Wednesday, November 3, after all voting stations had closed, (including those in Hawaii and Alaska), based on standard, network-funded exit polls through the National Election Pool (NEP), the leading pollsters and commentators showed a clear consensus that the electorate had given a victory to John Kerry and a defeat for George W. Bush.

Nationwide, the margin for Kerry appeared to be in the range of 1.5 million votes.

The apparent Kerry victory was also acknowledged in the Bush camp. Advisor Karen Hughes informed Bush that he had lost. The mood at Bush Headquarters until after midnight EST was grim, in light of what appeared to be an obvious defeat.

The Edison/Mitofsky nationwide poll was conducted independent of the state-by-state polls. It involved a national sample of 13,047 respondents, a sample roughly six times as large as is usually expected in such a poll. Later, citing a double-counting error, Mitofsky reported a corrected figure at 12,219. According to Mitofsky's own data, as calculated by U.S. Counts Votes, the odds of Bush winning, given the exit polls, were 1 in 16.5 million. The large sample size drove the margin of error down from the usual plus/minus 3% to plus/minus 1.1%, a very narrow range.

According to statisticians Ron Baiman and Jonathan Simon, the possibility that Kerry's reported official vote count of 48.1% was accurate was less than 1 in 959,000, a virtual statistical impossibility, based on the national Edison/Mitofsky poll. By contrast, it was 95% certain that Kerry's vote count was as high as 51.9% and no lower than 49.7%.

NOTES:

Bob Fitrakis, "Unanswered Exit Poll Questions," ColumbusAlive.com, November 16, 2000. This appears in "Essential Documents," p. 217.

Steven F. Freeman, "The Unexplained Exit Poll Discrepancy," A Research Report from the University of Pennsylvania;, December 29, 2004. See stfreeman@sas.upenn.edu.

Jonathan D. Simon and Ron P. Baiman, "The 2004 Presidential Election: Who Won the Popular Vote? An Examination of the Comparative Validity of Exit Poll and Vote Count Data," Freepress.org, January 2, 2004.

Steven F. Freeman, "Stolen or Lost," AlterNet, January 20, 2005.

Steven F. Freeman & Josh Mitteldorf, "A Corrupted Election: Despite What You May Have Heard, the Exit Polls Were Right," In These Times, February 15, 2005.

Ron Baiman, Affidavit, *Moss v. Bush*, op. cit.

4. *On a state-by-state basis, the Edison/Mitofsky and other major polling reports showed a strong correspondence between the exit polls and the official vote counts in 38 states plus the District of Columbia; but in Florida, Ohio and Pennsylvania, where the candidate who carried two of those three states would win, there were shifts of 4.9%, 6.7% and 6.5% from poll data to official tallies—all in favor of Bush, a virtual statistical impossibility.*

Overall, exit poll data in the rest of the US corresponded well with final official vote counts. Most importantly in Pennsylvania, Ohio and Florida, the variations between poll data and official outcome were significant, and highly unlikely.

In fact, of the eleven swing states, Wisconsin alone had a direct correlation between its exit polls and the official outcome. [Oregon, where the final vote count was also relatively close, is not included because it used mail-in votes and internet balloting that made exit polling impossible.]

But in the other ten swing states, all exit polls favoring Kerry shifted to official outcomes more favorable to Bush.

Most importantly, this happened in the three largest swing states, Pennsylvania, Ohio and Florida, where it was understood the candidate who carried two of the three would win. In Florida the shift from polls to final tally was 4.9% to Bush; in Ohio it was 6.7% to Bush; in Pennsylvania it was 6.5% to Bush. The odds on all this polling data shifting so significantly from Kerry to Bush in these three large states are statistically improbable.

NOTES:

Bob Fitrakis, "Unanswered Exit Poll Questions," ColumbusAlive.com, November 16, 2000. This appears in *Essential Documents*, p. 217.

Steven F. Freeman, "The Unexplained Exit Poll Discrepancy," A Research Report from the University of Pennsylvania;,

December 29, 2004. See stfreeman@sas.upenn.edu.

Jonathan D. Simon and Ron P. Baiman, "The 2004 Presidential Election: Who Won the Popular Vote? An Examination of the Comparative Validity of Exit Poll and Vote Count Data," Freepress.org, January 2, 2004.

Steven F. Freeman, "Stolen or Lost," AlterNet, January 20, 2005.

Steven F. Freeman & Josh Mitteldorf, "A Corrupted Election: Despite What You May Have Heard, the Exit Polls Were Right," *In These Times*, February 15, 2005.

Ron Baiman, Affidavit, *Moss v. Bush*, op. cit.

5. Exit polls vs. official tallies in four decisive swing states, show "purple" states originally going for Kerry but then shifting to Bush, giving Bush the presidency.

Exit polls on election night showed John Kerry winning 9 of 11 key swing states, and thus the Presidency of the United States. By morning, against all odds, Ohio, Iowa, Nevada and New Mexico had all shifted to Bush in the official vote count.

These four 'purple' states, which went from "blue" Kerry to "red" Bush are in italics. They gave Bush the presidency.

	Bush Predicted	Kerry Predicted	Predicted differential	Bush tallied	Kerry tallied	Tallied differential	Tallied vs. predicted
Colorado	49.9%	48.1%	Bush 1.8	52.0%	46.8%	Bush 5.2	Bush 3.4
Florida	49.8%	49.7%	Bush 0.1	52.1%	47.1%	Bush 5.0	Bush 4.9
Iowa	*48.4%*	*49.7%*	*Kerry 1.3*	*50.1%*	*49.2%*	*Bush 0.9*	*Bush 2.2*
Michigan	46.5%	49.7%	Kerry 5.0	47.8%	51.2%	Kerry 3.4	Bush 1.6
Minnesota	44.5%	51.5%	Kerry 9.0	47.6%	51.1%	Kerry 3.5	Bush 5.5
Nevada	*47.9%*	*49.2%*	*Kerry 1.3*	*50.5%*	*47.9%*	*Bush 2.6*	*Bush 3.9*
New Hampshire	44.1%	54.9%	Kerry 10.8	49.0%	50.3%	Kerry 1.3	Bush 9.5
New Mexico	*47.5%*	*50.1%*	*Kerry 2.6*	*50.0%*	*48.9%*	*Bush 1.1*	*Bush 3.7*
Ohio	*47.9%*	*52.1%*	*Kerry 4.2*	*51.0%*	*48.5%*	*Bush 2.5*	*Bush 6.7*
Pennsylvania	45.4%	54.1%	Kerry 8.7	48.6%	50.8%	Kerry 2.2	Bush 6.5
Wisconsin	48.8%	49.2%	Kerry 0.4	49.4%	49.8%	Kerry 0.4	No dif.

NOTES:

This table appeared on the CNN website, November 3, 2004, 12:30 am It appears in *Essential Documents*, p. 220.

6. The Election Night shift in the "purple" states of Ohio, Iowa, Nevada and New Mexico from exit poll victories for Kerry to official vote count victories for Bush is a virtual statistical impossibility.

As mentioned, the 12:21 am. exit polls showed Kerry carrying Ohio. They also showed him carrying Iowa, Nevada and New Mexico. These are the four "purple" states that started as "blue" for Kerry in the exit polls and ended "red" for Bush in the official vote count.

Winning Ohio in the official ballot count would have given Kerry the victory in the Electoral College.

The odds on any one of the above states going for Bush, individually, in contradiction to the findings of the exit polls that showed Kerry winning that state, are in the range of 100 to 1.

The odds on all four of the above states going for Bush in opposition to the findings of the exit polls in all those states are vanishingly small, i.e. a mathematical impossibility.

NOTES:

Bob Fitrakis, "Unanswered Exit Poll Questions," ColumbusAlive.com, November 16, 2000. This appears in *Essential Documents*, p. 217.

Steven F. Freeman, "The Unexplained Exit Poll Discrepancy," A Research Report from the University of Pennsylvania;, December 29, 2004. See stfreeman@sas.upenn.edu.

Jonathan D. Simon and Ron P. Baiman, "The 2004 Presidential Election: Who Won the Popular Vote? An Examination of the Comparative Validity of Exit Poll and Vote Count Data," Freepress.org, January 2, 2004.

Steven F. Freeman, "Stolen or Lost," AlterNet, January 20, 2005.

Steven F. Freeman & Josh Mitteldorf, "A Corrupted Election: Despite What You May Have Heard, the Exit Polls Were Right," *In These Times,* February 15, 2005.

Ron Baiman, Affidavit, *Moss v. Bush*, op. cit.

7. In the eleven swing states (with the exception of Wisconsin) discrepancies between exit polls and official vote counts all went in Bush's favor, a virtual statistical impossibility.

In the eleven swing states that were decided by less than seven percent of the vote, and that had become the focus of virtually the entire presidential campaign, there were significant discrepancies between the exit polling data and the official vote counts in all but Wisconsin. In Wisconsin, exit polls showed that Kerry would win by 0.4 percent of the vote, which he did in the official vote count.

But in the other ten swing states of Colorado, Florida, Iowa, Michigan, Minnesota, Nevada, New Hampshire, New Mexico, Ohio and Pennsylvania, all discrepancies between the exit polls and the final official vote count show the official vote count coming in higher for Bush than would have been indicated by the exit polls.

Overall, the final Bush official tallies came in higher than the exit poll tallies for him in these ten states, with margins in a range of 1.6 percent (Michigan) to 9.5 percent (New Hampshire).

No states that showed an exit poll victory for George W. Bush were reversed by the official ballot count into a victory for John Kerry. Four states that showed exit poll victories for John Kerry—Ohio, Iowa, Nevada and New Mexico—were reversed with the official vote counts, giving George W. Bush the presidency. These "purple" states gave Bush the presidency.

The odds on all official ballot counts going in the direction of a single candidate in significant contradiction to the state-of-the-art exit polling data in ten large voting venues as conducted in the United States in 2004 are vanishingly small, i.e., a statistical impossibility - except, as in Ukraine, for reasons of systematic irregularities, theft or fraud involving the official count. (John Zogby, president of the well-respected Zogby polling firm, told the Inter Press Service of Stockholm that "something is definitely wrong.") Political strategist Dick Morris wrote, "To screw up one exit poll is unheard of. To miss six of them is incredible. It boggles the imagination how pollsters could be that incompetent and invites speculation that more than honest error was at play here."

NOTES:

Bob Fitrakis, "Unanswered Exit Poll Questions," ColumbusAlive.com, November 16, 2000. This appears in *Essential Documents*, p. 217.

Dick Morris, "Those faulty exit polls were sabotaged," *The Hill*, November 13, 2005.

Steven F. Freeman, "The Unexplained Exit Poll Discrepancy," A Research Report from the University of Pennsylvania; December 29, 2004. See stfreeman@sas.upenn.edu.

Jonathan D. Simon and Ron P. Baiman, "The 2004 Presidential Election: Who Won the Popular Vote? An Examination of the Comparative Validity of Exit Poll and Vote Count Data," Freepress.org, January 2, 2004.

Steven F. Freeman, "Stolen or Lost," AlterNet, January 20, 2005.

Steven F. Freeman & Josh Mitteldorf, "A Corrupted Election: Despite What You May Have Heard, the Exit Polls Were Right," *In These Times*, February 15, 2005.

Ron Baiman, Affidavit, *Moss v. Bush*, op. cit.,

Bob Fitrakis, "How the Ohio Election was Rigged for Bush," Freepress.org, November 22, 2004.

8. As Election Night 2004 proceeded, the shift in projected vote counts from Kerry to Bush paralleled the shift from Gore to Bush in Florida 2000.

After midnight, the shift in the momentum in the vote count in the 2004 election paralleled the shift in 2000.

In 2000, network news teams began calling Florida and thus the general election for Al Gore. But, on insistence from a commentator at Fox News, (who was Bush's first cousin) and based on an apparent shift in the votes in Volusia County, the networks began to rescind their calls and to put Florida—and thus the election—in the questionable column.

As it turned out, the shift in the Volusia County vote tallies originated with a major computer error in Diebold machines. At some point in the vote count, the machines began to subtract votes from Al Gore while adding about 16,000 to Bush. When the running counts were figured into the overall Florida tally, they were enough to make it appear that Gore was now losing Florida, which was duly reported by all major news organizations. On the basis of this, Gore issued a preliminary concession.

But the glitch was discovered by an election worker who was mystified as to how Gore's tally could have gone down while the overall vote count had gone up. When the mistake was acknowledged, Gore retracted his concession. The official vote count showed him the winner nationwide by 500,000 votes.

But in Florida, a 36-day confrontation ensued which ended when the U.S. Supreme Court called a halt to the recount process and awarded the presidency to George W. Bush.

On Election Night 2004, polls again showed John Kerry with a significant lead. Network television screens showed the Democrat carrying Ohio, giving him a comfortable cushion in the Electoral College. Margins in Iowa, New Mexico and Nevada added to the lead.

By morning, the official vote count had shifted, and Kerry conceded. It was déja vu all over again.

NOTES:

Blackboxvoting.com, op. cit.

Greg Palast, *The Best Election Money Can Buy*, Bantam Books, Expanded Election Edition, 2004.

Bob Fitrakis, "Unanswered Exit Poll Questions," ColumbusAlive.com, November 16, 2000. This appears in "Essential Documents," p. 217.

Steven F. Freeman, "The Unexplained Exit Poll Discrepancy," A Research Report from the University of Pennsylvania; December 29, 2004. See stfreeman@sas.upenn.edu.

Jonathan D. Simon and Ron P. Baiman, "The 2004 Presidential Election: Who Won the Popular Vote? An Examination of the Comparative Validity of Exit Poll and Vote Count Data," Freepress.org, January 2, 2004.

Steven F. Freeman, "Stolen or Lost," AlterNet, January 20, 2005.

Steven F. Freeman & Josh Mitteldorf, "A Corrupted Election: Despite What You May Have Heard, the Exit Polls Were Right," *In These Times*, February 15, 2005.

Ron Baiman, Affidavit, *Moss v. Bush*, op. cit.

9. Kerry's concession came with outstanding issues in Ohio, New Mexico, Nevada and elsewhere unresolved, and with serious exit poll discrepancies still unexplained.

John Kerry's concession early November 3rd came with a wide range of issues unresolved in Ohio and elsewhere, and with exit poll data from the night before showing him to be the clear victor in the popular vote and—if accurate in Ohio, Nevada, New Mexico and Iowa—in the Electoral College, as well.

Kerry conceded with more than 93,000 Ohio ballots that were rejected by machine tabulators as yet uncounted. There were also some 155,000 provisional Ohio ballots still not tabulated. There were a number of spoiled ballots left to be dealt with. There were serious controversies in Warren and other counties still unresolved. There were massive, blatant issues of racial discrimination left hanging. And exit poll data still showed a popular victory for the challenger, as in Ukraine.

The Democrats apparently neither seriously considered requesting a recount in Ohio prior to conceding, nor did they participate in the demands that later forced one to take place, albeit in a manner deeply compromised by Secretary of State Blackwell.

Kerry's premature concession was the ultimate expression of passivity by a national party that seemed unwilling to fight for a presidential victory as hard as the opposition GOP. It showed a lack of commitment and fire amply reflected in the passivity of Ohio's Democratic Party officials and county Boards of Elections members. Overall, Ohio Democrats exhibited more commitment to forcing a true democratic outcome in Ukraine and the former Soviet Union than in Ohio and the United States.

NOTES:

Bob Fitrakis, "Unanswered Exit Poll Questions," ColumbusAlive.com, November 16, 2000. This appears in "Essential Documents," p. 217.

Steven F. Freeman, "The Unexplained Exit Poll Discrepancy," A Research Report from the University of Pennsylvania; December 29, 2004. See stfreeman@sas.upenn.edu.

Jonathan D. Simon and Ron P. Baiman, "The 2004 Presidential Election: Who Won the Popular Vote? An Examination of the Comparative Validity of Exit Poll and Vote Count Data," Freepress.org, January 2, 2004.

Steven F. Freeman, "Stolen or Lost," AlterNet, January 20, 2005.

Steven F. Freeman & Josh Mitteldorf, "A Corrupted Election: Despite What You May Have Heard, the Exit Polls Were Right," In These Times, February 15, 2005.

Ron Baiman, Affidavit, *Moss v. Bush*, op. cit.

10. The networks and Edison/Mitofsky exit pollsters refuse to make public their national, unadjusted raw data or to provide precinct identifiers.

Amidst major public demands to get to the bottom of the reasons for the discrepancies between exit polling and official ballot tallies, the networks and the lead Mitofsky/Edison polling organizations have locked up their raw data and refuse to allow it to be examined in the open media.

Mitofsky has released his **weighted adjusted data.** This purports to match Mitofsky's adjusted exit polls with Bush's official vote count.

But, Mitofsky's refusal to make his national, unadjusted raw data available, makes it impossible for independent analysts to determine whether Mitofsky's allegedly incorrect predictions of a Kerry victory are the result of a polling design or execution error, or something else. Moreover, his failure to provide precinct identifiers, even in blurred form to protect confidentiality, make it impossible for independent analysts to thoroughly investigate the validity of the pollsters' initial finding that George W. Bush actually lost the 2004 election.

NOTES:

Bob Fitrakis, "Unanswered Exit Poll Questions," ColumbusAlive.com, November 16, 2000. This appears in *Essential Documents*, p. 217.

Steven F. Freeman, "The Unexplained Exit Poll Discrepancy," A Research Report from the University of Pennsylvania;, December 29, 2004. See stfreeman@sas.upenn.edu.

Jonathan D. Simon and Ron P. Baiman, "The 2004 Presidential Election: Who Won the Popular Vote? An Examination of the Comparative Validity of Exit Poll and Vote Count Data," Freepress.org, January 2, 2004.

Steven F. Freeman, "Stolen or Lost," AlterNet, January 20, 2005.

Freeman & Mitteldorf, "A Corrupted Election...," op cit.

Ron Baiman, Affidavit, *Moss v. Bush*, op. cit.

Moss v. Bush, op. cit.

11. The four major lines of GOP attack on exit poll findings are unsubstantiated and unsupportable:

Assertion One: Differentiated time-of-day voting.

Under intense pressure from the GOP and conservative media outlets, just prior to the inauguration, Warren Mitofsky and associated pollsters questioned their own findings that Bush had lost the election. Such back-tracking is unprecedented in the history of exit polling. But it was much more limited than conservative major media indicated. Warren Mitofsky has been quoted as saying only that "we are still investigating the source of the exit poll problem," but has never renounced the findings of his company's 2004 surveys.

Undeterred, those intent on questioning the exit polls finding that John Kerry won the election of 2004 have focussed on four potential avenues.

To begin with, they wonder if Kerry voters might have come to the polls earlier in the day, while pro-Bush voters came later. Karl Rove and other Republican strategists encouraged this idea with equally unsubstantiated claims that massive numbers of evangelical voters responded to urgings from their church leaders to flood the polls in Florida and elsewhere late in the day against what appeared to be an evolving Kerry victory.

There is no hard evidence for any claim that more Bush supporters voted later in the day than Kerry voters.

NOTES:

Bob Fitrakis, "Unanswered Exit Poll Questions," ColumbusAlive.com, November 16, 2000. This appears in *Essential Documents,* p. 217.

Steven F. Freeman, "The Unexplained Exit Poll Discrepancy," A Research Report from the University of Pennsylvania;, December 29, 2004. See stfreeman@sas.upenn.edu.

Jonathan D. Simon and Ron P. Baiman, "The 2004 Presidential Election: Who Won the Popular Vote? An Examination of the Comparative Validity of Exit Poll and Vote Count Data," Freepress.org, January 2, 2004.

Steven F. Freeman, "Stolen or Lost," AlterNet, January 20, 2005.

Freeman & Mitteldorf, "A Corrupted Election...," op. cit.

Ron Baiman, Affidavit, *Moss v. Bush*, op. cit.

Moss v. Bush, op. cit.

---

12. The four major lines of GOP attack on exit polls findings are unsubstantiated and unsupportable:

Assertion Two: Differential poll access.

To refute exit poll findings that Kerry won the 2004 popular vote count, Bush supporters spun into the media allegations that pollsters were unable to gain access to certain polling stations, leading to a skewing of the data.

No hard evidence has been presented by the pollsters or the GOP indicating a lack of poll taker access (as opposed to international monitor access) during the election. Nor is there any evidence such an event might have happened in a way that would have explained the discrepancies in the exit poll outcomes versus the official vote counts. Nor is there any plausible explanation for how it might have happened in a way that would have changed the outcome of the exit polls.

NOTES:

Bob Fitrakis, "Unanswered Exit Poll Questions," ColumbusAlive.com, November 16, 2000. This appears in "Essential Documents," p. 217.

Steven F. Freeman, "The Unexplained Exit Poll Discrepancy," A Research Report from the University of Pennsylvania;, December 29, 2004. See stfreeman@sas.upenn.edu.

Jonathan D. Simon and Ron P. Baiman, "The 2004 Presidential Election: Who Won the Popular Vote? An Examination of the Comparative Validity of Exit Poll and Vote Count Data," Freepress.org, January 2, 2004.

Steven F. Freeman, "Stolen or Lost," AlterNet, January 20, 2005.

Steven F. Freeman & Josh Mitteldorf, "A Corrupted Election: Despite What You May Have Heard, the Exit Polls Were Right," *In These Times*, February 15, 2005.

Ron Baiman, Affidavit, *Moss v. Bush*, op. cit.

Moss v. Bush, op. cit.

13. The four major lines of GOP attack on exit poll findings are unsubstantiated and unsupportable:

Assertion Three: Gender bias.

GOP strategists have further asserted that poll takers may have gathered more responses from women, who favored Kerry, than from men, who favored Bush.

No hard evidence has been presented to back up this assertion. Nor is there any plausible reason to believe it is true.

Furthermore, all professional polls adjust for gender bias in their final accounting and track it closely. So any inequality between the number of men interviewed and the number of women would have been reported and accounted for in evaluating the raw data.

NOTES:

Bob Fitrakis, "Unanswered Exit Poll Questions," ColumbusAlive.com, November 16, 2000. This appears in *Essential Documents*,- p. 217.

Steven F. Freeman, "The Unexplained Exit Poll Discrepancy," A Research Report from the University of Pennsylvania;, December 29, 2004. See stfreeman@sas.upenn.edu.

Simon and Baiman, "The 2004 Presidential Election: ...," op. cit.

Steven F. Freeman, "Stolen or Lost," AlterNet, January 20, 2005.

Freeman & Mitteldorf, "A Corrupted Election: ...," op. cit.

Ron Baiman, Affidavit, *Moss v. Bush*, op. cit.

Moss v. Bush, op. cit.

14. The four major lines of GOP attack on exit poll findings are unsubstantiated and unsupportable:

Assertion Four: Democrats were more inclined to talk to exit poll worker than were Republicans.

A final hypothesis put forward by GOP spinners is the idea that Democrats were more willing to talk to pollsters than Republicans.

No hard evidence is put forward to substantiate this claim.

In fact, at least one study indicates that Republican precincts were over-represented in the exit polls as opposed to Democratic precincts, rather than under-represented, and that a higher percentage of Republicans were interviewed than Democrats.

Overall, there is no more hard evidence to indicate any extraordinary failings in the exit polls conducted for the 2004 presidential election in the United States than was found in Mexico 2000, the Philippines or any of the former Soviet republics, including Georgia and Ukraine. In all these latter cases, the exit polls were viewed to be at least as true and accurate as the official vote count.

NOTES:

Bob Fitrakis, "Unanswered Exit Poll Questions," ColumbusAlive.com, November 16, 2000. This appears in *Essential Documents*, p. 217.

Steven F. Freeman, "The Unexplained Exit Poll Discrepancy," A Research Report from the University of Pennsylvania;, December 29, 2004. See stfreeman@sas.upenn.edu.

Simon and Baiman, "The 2004 Presidential Election:...," op. cit.

Steven F. Freeman, "Stolen or Lost," AlterNet, January 20, 2005.

Freeman & Mitteldorf, "A Corrupted Election:...," op. cit.

Ron Baiman, Affidavit, *Moss v. Bush*, op. cit.

Moss v. Bush, op. cit.

Chapter Four:

The Vote Count

As the vote count unfolded the evening of November 2nd and beyond, widespread reports of unexplained and often bizarre anomalies, all of them favoring George W. Bush, surfaced in counties throughout Ohio, New Mexico and other states.

1. According to John Kerry, George W. Bush carried all New Mexico precincts equipped with electronic voting machines, regardless of the precinct's demographic make-up or political history.

After the election, in a teleconference with Rev. Jesse Jackson, co-author Bob Fitrakis and attorney Cliff Arnebeck, John Kerry confirmed that the election in New Mexico hung on the type of machine used to count the votes. Kerry said that he lost all precincts equipped with touchscreen DRE machines, regardless of the area's racial and ethnic make-up, its income levels or its voting history.

NOTES:

John Kerry, in a teleconference with Rev. Jesse Jackson, Bob Fitrakis, Cliff Arnebeck, et. al., November, 2004.

Bob Fitrakis, Steve Rosenfeld & Harvey Wasserman, "Ohio's Non-Recount Ends Amidst New Evidence of Fraud, Theft and Judicial Contempt in New Mexico," Freepress.org, December 31, 2004. This article appears in *Essential Documents*, p. 130.

2. In New Mexico, "phantom votes" in fifteen of thirty-three counties cloud the official vote count in a pivotal swing state.

In nearly half of New Mexico's counties, more votes were counted than were recorded as being cast. These "phantom votes," which totaled in the range of 2,000 for the state, have never been fully accounted for. They were dismissed by the Secretary of State's office as an "administrative lapse."

Though exit polls showed Kerry winning New Mexico, the official vote count gave the state to Bush by 1.1%, making it a "purple" state.

NOTES:

Warren Stewart, "What Are They Hiding in New Mexico," National Ballot Integrity Project," January 18, 2005. This appears in *Essential Documents*, p. 156.

Ellen Theisen, "Voters Unite!", Votersunite.org from "Myth Breakers: Facts About Electronic Elections," February, 2005. This appears in *Essential Documents*, op. cit., p. 297.

3. In New Mexico, undervotes accounted for 2.45% of the votes, more than double Bush's margin of victory in the state.

While phantom votes remain unaccounted for, New Mexico led the nation in undervotes - i.e. ballots cast without showing a presidential preference.

Representing 2.45% of the state's total official tally, undervotes accounted for more than twice as many ballots as officially decided the state for George W. Bush. New Mexico's Secretary of State said, "I'm just speculating that some voters are just not concerned with the presidential race."

NOTES:

Stewart, "What Are They Hiding...," op. cit.

Theisen, "Voters Unite!", op. cit.

4.   In Ohio, Kerry carried 54.46% of the votes counted by hand, as opposed to those counted by machine.

After Election Day in Ohio, some 147,400 provisional and absentee ballots were counted by hand. From the hand-counted ballots Kerry gained a 54.46% margin, a far higher percentage than from those ballots counted by machine.

NOTES:

Conyers Report, op. cit.

5.   In Franklin County, official vote tallies show white precincts with a 10% higher turnout than African-American precincts, reflecting voting machine and other procedural problems indicating a partisan effort to suppress the African-American vote.

In Franklin County, with white precincts reporting shorter lines to vote and an excess of voting machines, the final vote count indicated a turnout of 60.56%. But in African-American precincts, where there were voting machine and a wide range of other problems, including harassment and intimidation, official turnout was just 50.78%. According to researcher Richard Hayes Phillips, this gap is likely to have cost Kerry at least 17,000 votes just in Franklin County.

NOTES:

Phillips Report, op. cit.

6.   In Ohio, more than 106,000 machine-rejected and provisional ballots are known to have been disallowed and, thus, remain uncounted.

By official accounting from the Secretary of State's office, some 92,672 machine-rejected ballots remain uncounted. These are ballots that are most likely valid, but which could not be processed by mechanical tabulators.

At least 14,000 provisional ballots were also accounted for but left uncounted.

In sworn testimony taken after the election, observers charged that far more provisional ballots were simply discarded at the polling stations, without being accounted for. This allegation cannot be definitively confirmed or denied at this point, as the Secretary of State has refused to allow public perusal of the state's 2004 polling records, citing a still pending recent suit.

NOTES:

Phillips Report, op. cit.

CICJ Hearings Transcripts, op. cit.

7. Most uncounted ballots in Ohio came from districts that were strongest for Kerry.

According to research from Richard Hayes Phillips, the bulk of the machine-rejected and provisional ballots that came from Hamilton, Cuyahoga and Summit Counties came from precincts that went strongest for John Kerry.

NOTES:

Bob Fitrakis, Steve Rosenfeld & Harvey Wasserman, "Ten Preliminary Reasons Why the Bush Vote Does Not Compute, and Why Congress Must Investigate," Freepress.org, January 3, 2005. This article appears in *Essential Documents*, op. cit, p. 137.

Phillips Report, op. cit.

8. The "Loaves and Fishes" vote count in Gahanna, a Columbus suburb inside Franklin County, gave Bush an impossible tally.

At the Ward 1B precinct in Gahanna, a suburb of Columbus, 4,258 votes were tallied for George W. Bush where only 638 people were registered. The precinct was housed at the New Life Church, a fundamentalist congregation led by cohorts of the Rev. Jerry Falwell, a close associate of George W. Bush.

The glitch was blamed on a faulty electronic transmission, but was later dubbed the "loaves and fishes" vote count, in Falwell's honor.

NOTES:

Fitrakis & Wasserman, "How a Republican….," op. cit.

Fitrakis, Rosenfeld & Wasserman, "Ten Preliminary Reasons…," op. cit.

9. Two strongly pro-Bush precincts in Perry County initially reported official voter turnouts in excess of 100%.

Two heavily Republican Perry County precincts reported turnouts of 124.4% and 124.0% respectively. The vote count was heavily in favor of George W. Bush.

NOTES:

Bob Fitrakis, Steve Rosenfeld & Harvey Wasserman, "Ohio's Non-Recount Ends Amidst New Evidence of Fraud, Theft and Judicial Contempt in New Mexico," Freepress.org, December 31, 2004.

Conyers Report, op. cit.

10. The Vote Count in two strongly pro-Bush Miami County precincts reported impossibly high results.

The tallies in the Concord South and Southwest precincts of Miami County reported official turnouts of 94.27% and 98.6% respectively. The vote counts were strongly in favor of Bush.

For these extraordinarily high turnouts to have been accurate, all but ten of the 689 citizens registered in the Concord Southwest precinct would have had to have voted. But according to evidence taken after the election, Evan Davis and *Free Press* volunteers conducted a door-to-door survey of part of the precinct that turned up twenty five registered citizens in the precinct who swore they had not voted.

NOTES:

Bob Fitrakis, Steve Rosenfeld & Harvey Wasserman, "Ohio's Non-Recount Ends Amidst New Evidence of Fraud, Theft and Judicial Contempt in New Mexico," Freepress.org, December 31, 2004. This article appears in *Essential Documents*, p. 130.

11. A machine in Mahoning County registered a negative 25 million votes for John Kerry.

A faulty electronic voting machine in Mahoning County (Youngstown) showed John Kerry receiving a negative 25 million votes. The glitch was apparently corrected.

NOTES:

Dr. Werner Lange, "Kerry votes switched to Bush and ballots pre-punched for Bush," Freepress.org, December, 24, 2004.

12. After Warren County locked out media and independent observers, it awarded George W. Bush an additional 14,000 votes over his tally in 2000.

After locking out all media observers, the Republican executive director of the Warren County Board of Elections awarded Bush an extra 14,000 votes over the number of votes he carried in 2000 over Al Gore.

The result came with unmonitored election workers, supervised by a Republican executive director, using Triad machines to count punch card ballots.

NOTES:

Phillips Report, op. cit.

13. Warren, Butler and Clermont Counties gave Bush a total margin of victory over Kerry in excess of his entire margin in the state of Ohio.

In 2004, official tallies showed Bush beating John Kerry by a collective margin of 132,685 votes in Warren, Butler and Clermont Counties. Bush's margin in these three counties alone substantially exceeded his 118,775-vote margin of victory in the entire state.

NOTES:

Phillips Report, op. cit.

Moss v. Bush, op. cit.

See also Secretary of State J. Kenneth Blackwell's *Official Certified Results*.

14. Warren, Butler and Clermont Counties gave Bush a huge additional margin of victory over Kerry in 2004 versus what they gave Bush over Gore in 2000.

In 2000, Bush beat Al Gore in Warren, Butler and Clermont Counties by a total of just 95,575, even though Gore pulled out of the Ohio campaign three months before the election.

In 2004, Kerry contested Ohio to the bitter end. He had thousands of volunteers in these three counties.

But somehow, the official vote count in these three counties showed Bush beating Kerry in 2004 by a margin of 37,000 votes more than he received against Gore. That additional 37,000-vote margin accounted for nearly a third of Bush's official statewide margin in 2004.

According to researcher Phillips and others, it is highly improbable that the official vote count in these three counties is accurate.

NOTES:

Phillips Report, op. cit. This appears in *Essential Documents*, p. 139.

Bob Fitrakis, Steve Rosenfeld and Harvey Wasserman, "Ten Preliminary Reasons Why the Bush Vote Does Not Compute, and Why Congress Must Investigate," Freepress.org, January 2005. This article appears on page 137 of *Essential Documents*.

Moss. v. Bush, op. cit.

---

15. Warren, Butler and Clermont Counties recorded virtually impossible comparative vote tallies for the presidential race in comparison with the race for Chief Justice of the Ohio Supreme Court.

In Warren, Butler and Clermont Counties, George W. Bush outpolled Thomas Moyer, the Republican candidate for reelection as Chief Justice of Ohio's Supreme Court, by 109,866 votes to 68,407, a margin of 41,459 votes. The outcome was plausible, in part because the Supreme Court race appeared far down on the ballot from the presidential choices at the top. Thus, more voters would be expected to vote in the presidential race than in the one for Supreme Court.

But on the same ballot, C. Ellen Connelly, the Democratic candidate for Moyers' seat, substantially outpolled John Kerry. Her official vote count of was 61,559 votes to Kerry's 56,234.

That outcome is beyond implausible.

Connelly is an African-American woman from Cleveland with extremely limited funds who did not contest in Warren, Butler or Clermont Counties, counties that are very conservative and have very few African-American residents. Connelly was outspokenly pro-choice and in favor of allowing gay rights, which the voters of these three counties overwhelming rejected by approving Amendment One.

According to statistician Richard Hayes Phillips, who dissected the vote tallies in those counties on a precinct-by-precinct basis, there is no plausible explanation for an official vote count showing more votes for Connelly than for Kerry other than theft and fraud. By Phillips' account, the discrepancy indicates a shifting of as many as 15,000 votes from Kerry to Bush, creating a 30,000-vote boost for Bush.

NOTES:

Phillips Report, op. cit.. This appears in *Essential Documents*, p. 139.

Bob Fitrakis, Steve Rosenfeld and Harvey Wasserman, "Ten Preliminary Reasons Why the Bush Vote Does Not Compute, and Why Congress Must Investigate," Freepress.org, January 2005. This article appears in *Essential Documents*. p. 1370.

Moss. v. Bush, op. cit.

16 In accordance with the directive from Blackwell that poll records were to be kept secret from the public, Pickaway County officials ejected a volunteer election monitor who was attempting to view previously public voting records after the election.

Secretary of State Blackwell's edict that poll records should be kept from the public was rigorously enforced around the state. On November 12, ten days after the election, election volunteer Victoria Parks attempted to examine poll books in Pickaway County. She was given the books by the director of the Board of Elections.

However, upon inspection, Ms. Parks found that the poll book from precinct 1A in Circleville had no signatures as required by law.

The director then told Ms. Parks that upon orders from the Secretary of State, she would not be allowed to examine the books, which the director grabbed back into her possession. Ms. Parks left immediately.

NOTES:

Harvey Wasserman & Bob Fitrakis, "It's the People Versus the Party of Hate & Terror and the Party of Duck & Run," Freepress.org, December 1, 2004. This appears in *Essential Documents*, pp. 77-79.

CICJ Hearings Transcripts, op. cit.

---

17. In Trumbull County, a large inflation in the number of absentee ballot numbers remains unexplained.

In testimony given after the election, independent observers Werner Lange and Maggie Hagan found 200 precincts in Trumbull County where the number of absentee ballots counted exceeded the number of registered absentee voters identified in the poll books. Trumbull County apparently counted 650 more absentee votes than there were confirmed absentee voters. Taken across Ohio's 88 counties, that would indicate up to 65,000 unexplained absentee ballots.

As of this printing, Ohio's electoral records are still under official lock and key by order of Secretary of State Blackwell, so there is no way to investigate this possibility further.

NOTES:

Werner Lange, "Kerry Votes Switched to Bush and Ballots Pre-Punched for Bush," Freepress.org, December 24, 2004. This appears in *Essential Documents*, p. 112.

---

18. The third-party tally in at least three heavily Democratic Cleveland precincts is improbably high, at the expense of John Kerry.

In precinct 4F of Cuyahoga County, the official 2004 tally shows 215 votes for Constitution Law candidate Greg Paroutka, alongside 290 votes for John Kerry and 21 for George W. Bush.

The precinct is virtually all African-American. In 2000, it went 91% for Al Gore. In 2004, the surrounding precincts went overwhelmingly for John Kerry, with virtually no votes going to Paroutka. Statewide, Paroutka tallied less than one quarter of 1% of the total statewide votes cast. So the votes officially tallied for Paroutka in precinct 4F most likely were subtracted from votes actually cast for Kerry.

In three other Cuyahoga precincts, minor third party candidates got 86%, 92% and 98% of the vote, a virtual statistical impossibility. Some observers have compared these outcomes to the "Jews for Buchanan" phenomenon of Florida 2000.

NOTES:

Fitrakis, Rosenfeld & Wasserman, "Ten Preliminary Reasons....," op. cit. This appears in *Essential Documents*, p. 139.

19. Improbably low turnouts of less than 30% of registered voters reported in at least seven inner-city Cleveland precincts indicate significant losses of Kerry votes.

Official vote counts indicate an overall turnout in Cuyahoga County of about 60%. However, in seven heavily Democratic precincts, vote totals equaled a turnout of less than 30% of the voters registered in the precinct.

In precinct 6C, Kerry beat Bush by 45 votes to one, but the vote count represented just 7.1% of the voters registered there.

In precinct 13D, where Kerry received 83.8% of the vote, the number of votes counted represented just 13.15% of those registered to vote. In precinct 13F, where Kerry received 97.5% of the vote, the number of votes counted represented just 19.6% of those registered.

Five other inner-city precincts showed official turnouts of just 21.01%, 21.80%, 24.72%, 28.83% and 28.97%.

Seven entire wards reported turnouts of less than 50%.

But overall the county reported vote counts that represented a turnout of more than 60% of those registered.

NOTES:

Fitrakis, "How the Ohio Election Was Rigged for Bush," Freepress.org, November 22, 2004. This appears in *Essential Documents*, p. 46.

Fitrakis, Rosenfeld & Wasserman, "Ten Preliminary Reasons....," op. cit. This appears in *Essential Documents*, p. 139.

Phillips Report, op. cit.

20. Uncounted votes in Cuyahoga County were extraordinarily high in precincts carried with large margins by Kerry, costing Kerry votes.

According to a study by statistician Richard Hayes Phillips, in 165 Cleveland precincts won overwhelmingly by John Kerry (by a margin of 12:1 in the aggregate), 4% or more of the ballots cast went uncounted.

Elsewhere in Cuyahoga County, outside of Cleveland, Phillips found 19 precincts where 4% or more of the ballots cast went uncounted; 16 of those precincts were carried by Kerry (by a margin of 8:1 in the aggregate). Normally, uncounted votes are 2% or less of the total.

NOTES:

Phillips Report, op. cit.

21. The ratio of machine-rejected ballots to counted ballots in Cleveland was eight times as high as in outlying suburbs of Cuyahoga County.

According to a study by statistician Richard Hayes Phillips, about 5.91% of the ballots cast in the heavily Democratic city of Cleveland were rejected by mechanical tabulators and left uncounted.

In the more conservative Republican suburbs of Cuyahoga County, only 0.70% were machine-rejected.

NOTES:

Phillips Report, op. cit.

22. Cuyahoga County's official vote for Kerry may have been reduced by 22,000 votes.

According to Richard Hayes Phillips, who conducted a precinct-by-precinct study of the turnout in Cuyahoga County, numerous other precincts in heavily African-American wards show unexpectedly- and implausibly - light turnouts, indicating that many of the votes cast in those wards may not have been counted.

According to Phillips, the systematic reduction of vote tallies in heavily Democratic precincts, such as 6C, 13D and 13F, likely reduced Kerry's overall vote total by about 22,000 votes.

NOTES:

Phillips Report, op. cit.

23. Low official turnout numbers in Toledo may have cost Kerry 7,000 votes.

According to Phillips, the apparent low vote counts in Cleveland had their counterparts in Toledo. Phillips' study shows that there were 63 precincts in Toledo with less than 60% turnout, all of them heavily favoring Kerry. Eight of the precincts reported turnouts well under 50%, reflecting problems with broken voting machine, shortages and questionable vote counts. Phillips estimates the suppressed tallies in Toledo may have cost Kerry at least 7,000 votes.

NOTES:

Phillips Report, op. cit.

Fitrakis, Rosenfeld & Wasserman, "Ten Preliminary Reasons....," op. cit. This appears in *Essential Documents*, p. 139.

24. In contrast to inner-city precincts in Lucas County, 25 pro-Bush suburban Lucas County precincts showed turnout rates above 85%.

While official voter turnout rates in inner-city Toledo precincts showed turnouts of under 60%, turnouts in 25 white suburban precincts were over 84%. There were no reported voting machine shortages in the suburban precincts.

The inner-city precincts went heavily for John Kerry; the suburban precincts went heavily for George W. Bush.

NOTES:

Phillips Report, op. cit.

25. In Lucas County, the vote count for the Democratic candidate for U.S. Congress was improbably higher than the vote count for Kerry.

In Lucas County, where Democratic Congresswoman Marcy Kaptur won re-election in 2004, Kaptur outpolled John Kerry by 13,461 votes. The outcome is highly unlikely.

That outcome is especially unlikely given that the official vote count in Lucas County shows that 220,190 voters cast ballots for president versus 215,721 for Congress.

NOTES:

General Election Management Systems, *Official Reports.*

Phillips Report, op. cit.

26. In Montgomery County, 47 pro-Kerry precincts showed a high rejection rate, far in excess of the county as a whole.

According to Phillips, in 47 precincts in Montgomery County—41 of them in Dayton—more than 4.0% of the votes cast were left uncounted. John Kerry won all 47 precincts by an aggregate ratio of 7:1. In these 47 precincts the machine rejection rate was 5.16%, versus 1.31% for the rest of the county.

NOTES:

Phillips Report, op. cit. This appears in *Essential Documents*, p. 141.

27. In Hispanic Ward 13-0, an apparent low voter turnout indicates another likely loss of Kerry votes.

Ohio ballots were not bi-lingual, there were few, if any, booklets of instructions in Spanish, and few poll workers spoke Spanish or were trained to accommodate Spanish-speaking voters as mandated by Section 203 of the Voting Rights Act.

The result was a likely drop in Spanish-speaking voters, most of whom favored Kerry. In Cuyahoga's heavily Hispanic precinct 13-0, about 90% of the votes counted were for Kerry. But only 53 votes were officially tallied, representing just 21% of those registered to vote in the precinct.

Given language barriers and the lack of proper training for election workers in Hispanic precincts, it would appear likely that a high percentage of the ballots cast there were spoiled. Election monitors swear there were long lines and chaos.

NOTES:

Fitrakis, "How the Ohio….," op. cit. This appears in *Essential Documents*, p. 45.

28. At least 8,099 of 24,472 provisional ballots that were known to have been cast in Cuyahoga County were thrown out.

Approximately one-third of all provisional ballots cast in heavily-Democratic Cuyahoga County were trashed. Reasons given ranged from the improper completion of necessary forms to having been cast at the wrong precinct, the pitfall introduced by Secretary of State Blackwell.

NOTES:

Phillips Report, op. cit. This appears in *Essential Documents*, p. 143.

29. An additional 19,000 votes were recorded in Miami County after they reported 100% of the precincts' vote totals, adding an extra 13,000 votes to Bush.

On Election Night, GOP-controlled Miami County announced a total turnout of 31,620 votes, with a majority of about 66% favoring George W. Bush. Later, the Board of Elections added nearly 19,000 votes to the total, about 13,000 of which went to Bush. The second tabulation gave John Kerry precisely the same percentage, 33.92%, of the vote as the first one, a virtual statistical impossibility.

NOTES:

Moss v. Bush, op. cit.

---

30. Amidst a shortage of voting machines in Franklin County, two of the electronic machines that were deployed displayed "error" messages during the recount.

In sworn testimony after the election, Green Party observer Amy Kaplan reported that two electronic voting machines being used in Franklin County had faulty cartridges that generated error messages throughout the day. The County's Director, Matt Damschroder, had no explanation for what might have happened to the votes cast on those machines.

NOTES:

CICJ Hearings Testimony, op. cit.

---

31. In Mercer County, some 4,000 votes were "lost."

In Mercer County, voting machine errors showed that 289 people had cast punch card ballots, but only 51 were counted for president. Overall, the county's website seemed to indicate that about 4,000 votes had somehow disappeared from the system.

NOTES:

Mary Anne Saucier, "Lawsuit Before the Ohio Supreme Court," December 24, 2004. In *Essential Documents*, pp. 119-122.

Moss. v Bush, op. cit.

---

32. Montgomery County showed a presidential undervote rate in pro-Kerry precincts nearly twice as high as in pro-Bush precincts.

In Montgomery County (Dayton), undervotes for president—ballots that were cast with no apparent attempt to vote for president—were recorded at a rate of 2.8% of the ballots cast in the 231 precincts that supported John Kerry.

In the 354 precincts that supported Bush, the undervote rate was 1.6%.

NOTES:

Saucier, "Lawsuit Before the...," op. cit. In *Essential Documents*, pp. 119-122.

Moss. v Bush, op. cit.

Chapter Five:

The Recount

1. Ohio's Secretary of State repeatedly refused to testify under oath on the conduct of the election, even though he insisted there were no major problems.

While Secretary of State Blackwell wrote proudly of the "excellent job" that had been done in administering Ohio's election, he refused repeated invitations, and notices of deposition, to testify under oath as to how he administered the election. In particular, he ignored a notice of deposition served as part of a lawsuit filed by election protection attorneys challenging the seating of Ohio's electors for George W. Bush. Blackwell retaliated by having Ohio Attorney General Jim Petro file a sanctions motion against the attorney who filed the lawsuit. This sanctions motion was ultimately rejected by the Ohio Supreme Court.

Blackwell also refused an invitation from Republican Congressman Bob Ney (R-OH) to testify at a hearing in Washington. Only when Ney brought his committee to Columbus did Blackwell testify under oath. His appearance resulted in a nasty verbal altercation with Congresswomen Juanita Millander-McDonald (R-CA) and Stephanie Tubbs Jones (D-OH).

NOTES:

Bob Fitrakis, Steve Rosenfeld & Harvey Wasserman, "Ohio GOP Election Officials Ducking Notices of Deposition as Kerry Enters Stolen Vote Fray," Freepress.org, December 28, 2004. This article appears in *Essential Documents*, p. 123.

New York Times, "Blaming the Messengers," op. cit.

Jeremy Holden, "Moyer Declines to Sanction Attorneys for Election Challenge," *The Daily Reporter*, Columbus, Ohio, May 20, 2005, p. 1.

J. Kenneth Blackwell, interview with Harvey Wasserman, January 26, 2005.

Harvey Wasserman, "Ohio's Secretary of State Blackwell Slanders Election Protection Attorney at Junket Sponsored by Voting Machine Vendors," Freepress.org. January 27, 2004.

2. Blackwell fiercely resisted a recount and rendered it meaningless.

After the election, as the Green Party and Libertarian Party filed suit for a lawful recount, Blackwell resisted, charging it was "unnecessary" and "a waste of money." The two parties—without the help of the Democrats—raised over $100,000 to force the recount.

Rev. Jesse Jackson, among others, argued that amidst such controversy, the Secretary of State should have welcomed a recount, especially if he had "nothing to hide."

But Blackwell's office resisted the recount at every point. With access to voting records denied, with extensive tampering with voting machines by private companies, with ballots left strewn about unsecured, and with a wide range of other problems - both intentional and otherwise - the recount was rendered meaningless.

NOTES:

Rainbow/PUSH Coalition, "Rainbow/PUSH Coalition Remains Committed to Investigation and Recount Efforts in Ohio," December 29, 2004. This document appears in *Essential Documents*, p. 126.

Statement of National Voting Rights Institute, Common Cause, Demos, Fannie Lou Hamer Project, and People for the American Way Foundation. This statement appears in *Essential Documents*, pp. 499-514. Hereafter referred to as *NVRI Statement*.

3. Blackwell postponed official certification of the balloting so the recount could not be done until after the state's electors had convened and cast their ballots for George W. Bush.

Under Ohio law, the recount could not begin until the Secretary of State officially certified the vote count. Blackwell arbitrarily delayed that certification so the recount could not be finished prior to the convening of Ohio's electors, whom Blackwell certified for Bush at the earliest possible moment.

NOTES:

Bob Fitrakis, Steve Rosenfeld & Harvey Wasserman, "Ohio's Non-Recount Ends Amidst New Evidence of Fraud, Theft and Judicial Contempt in New Mexico," Freepress.org, December 28, 2004.

Conyers Report, op. cit.

NVRI Statement, op. cit.

4. In Greene County, ballots were left unguarded on folding tables in an open building after the election, compromising the recount.

According to sworn testimony given after the election, independent observers found hundreds of ballots lying open and unguarded, strewn atop folding tables in a public building whose doors were not locked. The ballots' easy accessibility to theft and fraud made the recount in Greene County a meaningless charade.

NOTES:

CICJ Hearings Transcripts, op. cit.

5. Contrary to Ohio law, Blackwell barred independent observers from gaining access to polling books.

In direct defiance of Ohio law, representatives of the Green Party and Libertarian Party, who paid for a recount of Ohio's presidential tally, were denied full access to poll books which might have shed light on widespread allegations of theft and fraud. Those allegations were vehemently denied by Blackwell, but they did not prompt him to open the books, which remain shut to this day, again in defiance of Ohio election law.

NOTES:

CICJ Hearings Transcripts, op. cit.

NVRI Report, op. cit.

6. Contrary to Ohio law, precincts to be recounted were not blindly chosen at random, as required, but rather were consciously selected by those doing the recounts, seriously compromising the validity of the recount.

Under Ohio law, a recount requires the hand counting of 3% of the ballots cast, done county-by-county. The precincts in which the votes are to be recounted are to be hand picked at "random," meaning all have an equal chance at inclusion.

But according to sworn testimony given after the election, numerous county Boards of Elections around the state chose to make their 3% quotas by recounting specific precincts. The precincts were deliberately chosen. Criteria for choosing a precinct to count varied. Put simply: without random selection of the votes to be recounted, there was no legal recount in Ohio.

NOTES:

NVRI Report, op. cit.

CICJ Hearings Transcripts, Lucas County, op. cit.

7. At least one county election board discarded key equipment and data prior to the recount, compromising its accuracy.

In response to a Freedom of Information request signed by co-author Harvey Wasserman, Shelby and other counties confirmed that they had destroyed key components of voting machines before the recount could take place. The destruction may have been illegal. The recount was, thus, fatally compromised.

NOTES:

Shelby County Board of Elections, Letter to Harvey Wasserman, December 2, 2004.

8. During the recount, Triad got access to Hocking County's central tabulator.

In Hocking County, an unscheduled Triad operative gained access to voting machines after the election, but before the recount. When the intrusion was made public by Sherole Eaton, the Deputy Director of the Board of Elections, she was fired.

NOTES:

Conyers Report, op. cit. Affidavit of Sherole Eaton, December 13, 2004. This appears in the appendix of *Essential Documents*.

9. In New Mexico, recount efforts were successfully resisted by Democratic Governor Bill Richardson, and no recount has taken place.

Exit polls showed John Kerry winning New Mexico. Unexplained "phantom" overvotes and thousands of undervotes tainted the official outcome. Kerry himself confirmed that he had lost all precincts that had electronic voting machines, no matter what the demographic or political make-up of the precinct itself.

Nonetheless, New Mexico's Democratic Governor Bill Richardson fought off a grassroots movement demanding a recount. Through strenuous legal maneuvering and stiff financial requirements, Richardson made it impossible for a meaningful public accounting of the state's balloting to proceed.

To this date, there has been no recount of the New Mexico vote, which, according to the exit polls, should have gone to John Kerry.

NOTES:

Stewart, "What are They Hiding…," op. cit. This appears in *Essential Documents*, p. 156.

PART TWO:

HOW THE GOP
IS RIGGING 2008

Chapter Six:

Making Election Theft Permanent

1. The Republican Party has pushed through the states of Indiana and Georgia, and is pushing in Ohio and elsewhere, laws requiring photo identification to vote, a measure that could disenfranchise millions of elderly, poor and non-white citizens, and could have a significant impact on all future elections.

Indiana and Georgia have passed laws requiring photographic identification for voting, a requirement *The New York Times* and others believe to be in violation of the Voting Rights Act of 1965, having "the effect of denying or abridging the right to vote on account of race." Under federal law the Department of Justice can reject these laws, but as the Republican Party is the primary beneficiary, a rejection is unlikely to occur under the Bush Administration.

The Ohio and other Republican-controlled legislatures are pushing similar legislation, even though Georgia's Secretary of State, Cathy Cox, has said she cannot recall any cases of anyone attempting to impersonate a voter. It is estimated that 150,000 older Georgians who voted in 2004 are without driver's licenses, as are thousands more who are poor or without cars. Across the country, Hispanics, African-Americans and other citizens of color are far less likely to have photo identification than whites. State-by-state such legislation would have a clear and powerful impact in swaying future elections toward the Republican Party.

Among other things, the law would effectively prevent from voting many Americans who harbor a principled opposition to such identification papers.

Rev. Jesse Jackson has denounced such legislation as an extension of the Jim Crow discrimination that defined southern politics after the Civil War. *The New York Times* editorialized that such a law has "no place in a democracy."

But in the broader context of all else that has happened to the American electoral system, it may be that democracy cannot survive such a law.

NOTES:

Ariel Hart, "Georgia Voters May Soon Need Photo ID's," *New York Times*, p. 15A, April 1, 2005.

New York Times, "Georgia's Undemocratic Voter Law," Editorial Page, July 20, 2005.

2. Immediately after the 2004 election, the Ohio Legislature passed an Omnibus Bill, HB-1, greatly skewing the electoral funding process in favor of the Republicans, and likely serving as a template for laws to be pushed by Republicans in other states.

The HB-1 bill passed by the Republican-dominated Ohio legislature in a special December 2004 lame duck session may make it virtually impossible for Democrats ever to gain control of the Ohio legislature again.

Parts of the bill are certain to surface in other Republican-controlled legislatures around the country.

NOTES:

House Bill One, page 95: www.legislature.state.oh.us\ Hereafter referred to as *HB-1.*

3. HB-1 opens the door to direct corporate contributions to political parties.

Under the Republican President Theodore Roosevelt roughly a century ago, the United States government banned direct corporate contributions to political parties.

HB-1 restricts donations directly to candidates, but does allow corporations to sponsor everything that surrounds a political campaign, including polling, get-out-the-vote campaigns and the like.

NOTES:

HB-1, op. cit.

4. HB-1 quadruples the amount of money individual donors can contribute to political parties.

Under HB-1, individual contributors may now give $10,000 to political campaigns in each Ohio election cycle. The previous limit was $2500.

HB-1 also allows family members over the age of six to contribute $10,000 each. Hence, a family of four may give $40,000 in the primary, and $40,000 in the general elections.

NOTES:

HB-1, op. cit.

5. HB-1 would severely restrict the ability of labor unions to impact statewide elections.

HB-1 includes a series of restrictions on union activity which severely curtails organized labor's ability to impact statewide elections.

These restrictions also make it unlikely any party other than the Republicans will dominate the Ohio legislature in the future.

The AFL-CIO, AFSCME and SEIU have sued, and as of this writing have won a stay on implementation of these restrictions. But the final outcome is still uncertain.

NOTES:

Tim Burka, Ohio AFL-CIO, Interview with Harvey Wasserman, August 22, 2005.

Catherine Turcer, Ohio Citizen Action, Interview with Harvey Wasserman, August 19, 2005.

HB-1, op. cit.

For filings, see www.ohaflcio.org.

6. The Republican extremely repressive proposed House Bill 3 (HB-3) passed the Ohio House in early 2005, and, though it has not yet passed the Ohio Senate, is likely to pass there and to serve as a template for bills to be pushed nationwide by the GOP.

In early 2005, the Republican-dominated Ohio House passed HB-3, an extremely repressive Omnibus Bill designed to disenfranchise largely Democratic voters.

Similar legislation is likely to surface in Republican-dominated legislatures around the country.

NOTES:

Proposed HB-3. is at www.legislature.state.oh.us. Hereafter referred to as *Proposed HB-3.*

---

7. Proposed HB-3 would codify a broad range of limitations on voter registration, making it much harder for average citizens to vote and, thus, for any effective challenge to GOP control of Ohio.

The extremely repressive omnibus House Bill 3 was proposed in the Ohio Legislature in early 2005 and passed by the Ohio House. Its various provisions, when combined with the financial advantages given the GOP in HB-1, would make it virtually impossible for the Democratic Party to ever carry Ohio again.

No modern candidate except John Kennedy has won the presidency without carrying Ohio. Because of Ohio's pivotal nature in presidential elections, the various provisions of these two bills, plus additional restrictions in the wings, could virtually guarantee permanent GOP control of the U.S. Executive Branch.

NOTES:

Proposed HB-3, op. cit.

---

8. Under proposed HB-3, an individual citizen or a voter registration worker must return a voter registration form to the county in which the voter is registered, rather than to a central location, for processing.

Under current law, Ohioans may register outside the counties where they are registered to vote. Volunteer or professional registration workers may also submit new registration forms to locations outside the counties in which those wishing to register will vote.

Under proposed HB-3, if you wish to register to vote, you must do so in your home county. And if you register with a registration worker, that worker must submit your form in your home county.

The effect of this provision is to make it much harder for Ohioans to register to vote. It would virtually kill voter registration drives. Especially hard hit would be college campuses, where students come from all the state's 88 counties.

Proposed HB-3 would make it a felony to return a registration form to the wrong county.

NOTES:

Proposed HB-3, op. cit.

9. Under proposed HB-3, paid voter registration workers would be required to register themselves in every county in which someone they register to vote may cast their ballot, severely impairing statewide voter registration drives.

Under this bill, paid voter registration workers would be required to register themselves with each and every county in which someone they register will vote. This will make voter registration drives virtually impossible on college campuses, the state fair and elsewhere around the state.

NOTES:

Proposed HB-3, op. cit.

---

10. Under proposed HB-3, paid registration workers may be required to undergo yearly trainings in every county from which someone they register may vote.

Signing up to register voters from a county may come with a requirement to do an annual training. Should paid voter registration agents be required to train each year in the counties in which the people they register will vote, Statewide voter registration drives may become a virtual impossibility.

NOTES:

Proposed HB-3, op. cit.

---

11. Institutional employees working where voter registration forms are distributed, such as banks, may be required under proposed HB-3 to sign up with the counties in which those who register in their institution may vote.

Many banks and other public institutions regularly distribute voter registration forms. Under HB-3, tellers and other employees of businesses where forms are distributed may be forced to register themselves and undergo training in the counties in which those who sign up will vote. This will make such general distribution of voter registration cards virtually impossible.

NOTES:

Proposed HB-3, op. cit.

---

12. Under proposed HB-3, county Boards of Election will send out cards informing voters that they are registered, and where they are to vote, but if the card is returned for any reason, voters will be required to show identification at the polling station, and will be allowed only a provisional ballot.

Under proposed HB 3, the county Boards of Elections will mail every registered voter a post card prior to every election in an even-numbered year, which includes Congressional, Senatorial and Presidential elections. The card will tell the citizen where to vote.

But if the card is returned for any reason, the voter cannot get a regular ballot. S/he must show identification at the polling station, and must then vote with a provisional ballot, which requires substantial additional time and paperwork. This will make it virtually impossible for the homeless to vote, and will have a major impact on the elderly and poor.

NOTES:

Proposed HB-3, op. cit.

13. Under proposed HB-3 (mirroring HAVA requirements) if a citizen registers by mail, and fails to include a copy of a driver's license or other designated ID, only a provisional ballot can be issued at the polling station.

Under current law, after registering by mail without providing a copy of ID in the envelope, a citizen can vote with a regular ballot with current ID.

Under proposed HB-3, even with proper ID at the polling station, only a provisional ballot will be made available.

Because of widespread concerns about identity theft, many citizens are now unwilling to put copies of their ID in the mail. Many elderly and poor people either do not have photo ID, or would be unable or disinclined to find a place to copy what they have.

Though this mirrors the federal HAVA Act, HB-3 would once again disenfranchise thousands of Ohioans.

NOTES:

Proposed HB-3, op. cit.

14. The proposed requirement that voters provide photo identification amounts to a poll tax.

Because photo identification can cost money to obtain, the requirement that it be present to obtain a ballot amounts to a poll tax. *The New York Times* and others have suggested that this is a discriminatory edict.

NOTES:

New York Times, "Georgia's Undemocratic Voter...," op. cit.

Proposed HB-3, op. cit.

15. Under proposed HB-3, if a voter changes his/her name or moves even within his/her home precinct, only a provisional ballot will be issued at the next election.

Currently a citizen may vote within his/her precinct with a regular ballot after a change of name and/or address. Proposed HB-3 would stop that and demand that only a provisional ballot be provided.

NOTES:

Proposed HB-3, op. cit.

16. Under proposed HB-3, obtaining an absentee ballot will require presenting designated ID at the Board of Elections, or enclosing a copy with the application.

Currently, Ohioans are not required to show ID when obtaining an absentee ballot. Proposed HB-3 would change that.

NOTES:

Proposed HB-3, op. cit.

17. Many GOP politicians say they will continue to move to require photo ID under all circumstances to vote.

Though not now required, and not part of HB-3, GOP leaders have made clear their intent to require photo identification at all polling stations. Such laws are now in place in Georgia and Indiana. They have the effect of radically reducing the ability of the elderly and poor to vote.

NOTES:

Catherine Turcer, Interview, Ohio Citizen Action, with Harvey Wasserman, August 19, 2005.

18. GOP politicians indicate they will move to ban ex-felons from voting in Ohio.

Republican state senators indicate they will work to ban ex-felons from voting in Ohio. This measure, which heavily discriminates against young, poor and non-white voters, was put in place mostly in the former Confederacy after the Civil War to deprive ex-slaves of the vote. The law in Florida was almost certainly responsible for putting George W. Bush in the White House in 2000. An estimated 31% of Florida's black males were deprived of the right to vote by this law, representing far more than enough votes to have turned the election to Al Gore.

Current Ohio law bans from voting felons currently in prison. But those who are freed, awaiting trial or in half-way houses may vote.

In Ohio 2004, the County Board of Elections sent letters to 34,000 citizens telling them they could not vote because they were ex-felons. This letter deliberately misstated Ohio law. It also went to many Ohioans who were not actually ex-felons, canceling their legitimate right to vote.

As in Florida 2000, the ban on ex-felon voting was used as a pretext to send letters to thousands of citizens who had been convicted of no crime, but whose names were vaguely similar to ex-felons. The list of those who received such letters was disproportionately African-American and Democratic. Its use may well have decided the 2000 election, and could decide future elections in Ohio and elsewhere.

NOTES:

Ohio Rep. Dan Stewart (D-Columbus), Interview with Bob Fitrakis, June 24, 2005.

19. Proposed HB-3 would raise the charge for conducting a statewide recount from $10/precinct to $50/precinct.

Political parties are currently required to pay for statewide recounts at the rate of $10/precinct. In 2004, the Green and Libertarian Parties raised roughly $110,000, to recount Ohio's 11,000-plus precincts.

HB-3 would raise that price by a factor of five, making recounts far less affordable. Most likely, the price would have prevented the Green/Libertarian supporters from funding the recount in 2004. It could also effectively deprive the American public of future recounts in the nation's most pivotal swing state.

NOTES:

Proposed HB-3, op. cit.

20. Proposed HB-3 would ban, under Ohio law, any challenge to a federal-level election conducted in the state.

The bitterly contested 2004 election in Ohio was challenged by the *Moss v. Bush* lawsuit. As a result, much of the core information about the election was put into the public record which otherwise would not have been made public, or been available for the historical record.

In retaliation, Secretary of State Blackwell moved to have sanctioned the lawyers who filed the lawsuit. The Ohio Supreme Court eventually refused the attempt.

Under HB-3, lawsuits challenging federal-level elections conducted in Ohio would be banned by law. The ban has been passed by the Ohio House of Representatives, and could be made law by the Senate.

NOTES:

Proposed HB-3, op. cit.

Jeremy Holden, "Moyer Declines to Sanction Attorneys for election challenge," *The Daily Reporter,* May 20, 2005.

21. In the summer of 2005, the Ohio GOP proposed an extremely repressive state version of the federal Patriot Act that would have severely curtailed freedom of speech, academic freedom and a wide range of rights and liberties that might well have made future elections moot, and still could, both in Ohio and nationwide.

In the summer of 2005, the Ohio Legislature temporarily tabled an extremely repressive statewide GOP version of the federal Patriot Act. This legislation would have severely curtailed a wide range of freedoms and liberties in Ohio, eviscerating the Bill of Rights.

The bill was temporarily tabled. But its backers have pledged to bring it back. It is also likely to serve as a template for similar versions to be introduced by the GOP to state legislatures around the U.S. Such laws would make future elections on any level in this country virtually moot.

Given the track record of the Bush/Rove-era GOP, it is unlikely the temporary tabling of this bill in Ohio will deter them from bringing it back until they pass all or most of it. A future terror attack might also be used as a pretext to getting it passed.

NOTES:

Jon Craig, "Ohio Bill Adds Terror-Fighting Tool: Getting ID's Would be Tougher Under State Patriot Act," *Cincinnati Enquirer*, June 13, 2005.

"Ohio Patriot Act Vote Postponed," American Civil Liberties Union of Ohio, ACLU.org, August 4, 2005.

Sub. S.B. No.9: www.legislature.state.oh.us

22. After the 2004 election, Franklin County Board of Elections Director Matt Damschroder stripped county voter rolls of more than 100,000 registered voters.

In the months following the 2004 election, Republican BOE Director Damschroder followed Hamilton County's lead in stripping more than 100,000 registered voters from Franklin County's voter list. This drastic reduction almost certainly included many thousands of heavily Democratic African-American voters, and will make it more difficult for Democrats in the 2006 and 2008 elections.

NOTES:

Robert Vitale, "Number of New Voters Soaring," *Columbus Dispatch*, October 1, 2004. P. 1D.

Robert Vitale, "County Shrinks Its Pumped-Up Voter Rolls: Standard Housecleaning Chops Nearly 114,000," *Columbus Dispatch*, June 27, 2005.

Niquette, "G.O.P. Stronghold...," op. cit.

Chapter Seven:

What's With the Democrats?

1.   In the lead-up to the Ohio election, Franklin County Democrats failed to fight for paper ballots and for equal access to the polls.

In Franklin County, Democrats understood that severe access problems were likely to occur in heavily Democratic inner-city wards. Ed Leonard, the former Democratic Deputy Director, warned the Board of Elections in a 2001 memo entitled "Parting Thoughts" that there were very likely to be such problems in the future.

Franklin County Democratic Chair Bill Anthony, also Chair of the Franklin County Board of Elections, quietly asked Secretary of State Blackwell to allow distribution of paper ballots, which might have solved at least part of the problem, shortened lines and avoided the disenfranchisement of tens of thousands of Democratic voters.

Anthony did not make the request public. Nor did he make a public protest, or take any other action when Blackwell rejected the request. The public may have first heard what happened when Anthony admitted to the episode on separate radio shows with co-authors Harvey Wasserman and Bob Fitrakis, well after the election had taken place.

2.   Franklin County Democrats, and Democrats in other counties around the state, stood quietly by while the GOP deprived inner-city wards of voting machines, disenfranchising thousands of African-Americans and costing the Democrats thousands of votes, and possibly the presidential election.

Anthony and other Franklin County Democrats watched quietly, without protest, while Republican Director Matt Damschroder systematically deprived heavily Democratic inner-city wards of voting machines, costing the Democrats tens of thousands of votes.

Anthony and the Ohio Democratic Party later downplayed the impact of the manipulation of the voting machines.

The formula used by Director Damschroder, the former Chair of the Franklin County Republican Party, allocated voting machines based on "active voters." This formula failed to take into consideration the abundance of newly-registered voters in the inner-city, since "active voters" meant only past voters. But the Democrats did not object.

3.   On the morning of November 3rd, John Kerry conceded an election the exit polls showed he had almost certainly won.

As of 12:20 am. on November 3rd, exit polls with almost universal credibility showed John Kerry winning the presidency, both in the popular vote and in the Electoral College. By morning Kerry had conceded an election that, based on the exit polls, would have been as thoroughly rejected by the international community as was the vote in Ukraine a few months prior.

The exit polls showed Kerry winning both the popular vote nationwide and the Electoral College on the strength of having carried Ohio. Iowa, Nevada and New Mexico were also in Kerry's exit poll column. In Ohio, nearly 250,000 votes remained uncounted against an official Bush margin of less than 136,000 votes, later reduced to 118,000 after certification. No credible recount has ever been done in Ohio or New Mexico.

4. Democrats and pundits wrongly cite Richard Nixon's 1960 concession to John F. Kennedy amidst the apparent theft of Illinois as an act of statesmanship to be emulated.

Both Al Gore in 2000 and John Kerry 2004 were urged to concede quickly by pundits who argued they should follow the lead of Richard Nixon. Nixon conceded to John Kennedy in 1960 despite questions about that year's vote count in Chicago.

The Republicans have widely—and falsely—marketed Nixon's concession as an act of statesmanship, sparing the country a long, ugly stalemate that might have ensued while a disputed election could be sorted out. It was said, and is still being said, that Nixon put the country's interest ahead of his own by "allowing" JFK to become president without an Illinois challenge.

Chicago—and thus Illinois—may indeed have been stolen for the Democrats in 1960. But Illinois' 27 electoral votes were not sufficient to have swung the election for the Republicans. Kennedy won the Electoral College 303 to 219. Had Nixon fought it out and won Illinois in 1960, he still would have lost in the Electoral College by a margin of 276 for Kennedy to 246 for the GOP.

Some Republicans at the time claim the Democrats also stole New Jersey, which, in tandem with Illinois, could have given Nixon the presidency. But nothing serious came of the assertion, then or in ensuing years.

Thus, Nixon's concession was an inevitability, no matter what happened in Illinois. Few who knew Nixon or who have studied his career doubt that, had the election actually been at stake, he would have fought to the bitter end to challenge and switch Illinois' electoral votes.

But in 2000 and 2004, Florida and Ohio were both decisive. Had Gore fought for and won Florida in 2000, George W. Bush would not have become president. Had Kerry fought for and won Ohio in 2004, Bush would not have gotten a second term.

The 2004 exit polls showed Kerry winning Ohio, Iowa, Nevada and New Mexico, all of which went for Bush in the official vote count. Bush thus won the Electoral College by 286 to Kerry's 251. (One Minnesota elector voted for John Edwards for both president and vice president.)

In 2004, Ohio had twenty electoral votes, Iowa seven, Nevada five and New Mexico five. Had Ohio gone for Kerry, he would have won the presidency 271 to 266. Had Iowa, Nevada and New Mexico all gone for Kerry, but not Ohio, Bush would have had 269 to Kerry's 268, and then the one for Edwards. (What might that Minnesota elector have done then?)

5. With vote counts still in bitter dispute in Ohio, New Mexico and elsewhere, Kerry's concession represented an abandonment of his promise to guarantee that "every vote will be counted."

When Kerry conceded, bitter disputes were still unresolved over vote counts in Warren, Lucas, Mahoning, Franklin and other counties around Ohio involving more than enough votes to swing the election to the Democrats. Thousands of machine-rejected ballots and provisional ballots remained uncounted. The highly dubious vote counts from Warren County, where a Homeland Security alert had been conjured, were still unexamined. The ballots from Greene County, found scattered on unguarded tables, were still unexplained. Official low turnouts in Cuyahoga County indicated discarding of votes. In Hocking County, the central tabulator was left open to unsupervised computer technicians. And more…. In short, by all serious accounts, the election was anything but decided.

Similar disputes still surround undelivered absentee ballots in Florida, and phantom votes, mysterious undercounts, and suspicious touchscreen DRE tabulating patterns in New Mexico, among other things.

When Kerry conceded, he cited statements from his advisors alleging that there were not enough votes in Ohio in dispute to overcome the apparent margin for George W. Bush.

At the very least, this statement was profoundly in error.

6. Kerry's concession killed media attention to the irregularities, fraud and theft that defined the Ohio election, and thus may have allowed many votes to go undocumented.

Kerry's concession killed the "story" of the 2004 election as it was being played out in the major media, i.e. as a contest between him and George W. Bush for the presidency. Once Kerry abandoned ship, the world's scrutiny of what really happened in Ohio simply disappeared.

But more than enough has already been discovered to throw the 2004 election under a permanent cloud of suspicion and doubt. Ohio 2004 has been, after all, the only entire state electoral delegation ever challenged in the U.S. Congress.

Had Kerry stood and fought, the world media almost certainly would have camped in Columbus, as it did in Florida 2000. With the race still in doubt, and with the media's huge resources focused on the story, it's reasonable to believe that far more would have surfaced than what we have been able to present in this and other books, articles and writings with virtually no money and a dedicated but limited crew of grassroots volunteers.

Indeed, Kerry's premature concession marginalized the truest democrats of them all, the grassroots activists still fighting to get to the bottom of what really happened in Ohio. The refusal of the Democratic Party to contribute even minimal resources to that struggle has not helped. Its astonishing attacks on those true patriots who have continued to dig have made things worse.

7. Kerry's quick concession will almost certainly discourage Democratically-inclined citizens from turning out to vote again in 2008.

The Democratic Party's indifference and hostility to issues of GOP intimidation, manipulation, theft and fraud will obviously make it harder for future Democratic candidates to be taken seriously. Kerry's abandonment of his very public, very well-funded commitment to count every vote will be hard for many to forget in 2008, particularly the thousands of volunteers who poured into Ohio and other swing states to save the republic from more of George W. Bush.

It will take some very hard work to persuade the hundreds of thousands of African-American, Hispanic, student and other voters—many of them first-timers—who were turned away at the polls in 2004 to come back in 2008.

Who among those who suffered through long, racially tainted lines in the cold November rain only to have their votes trashed and their rights abandoned will be inclined to work with fervor for another Democrat?

Indeed, having been abandoned in 2004, minority voters may already have been effectively disenfranchised by the tens of thousands for 2008. Should new voter ID requirements be thrown into the mix, along with further GOP campaign finance manipulations and unregulated electronic voting machines, it may well be that the 2008 election has already been decided.

8. Kerry raised $7 million specifically to guarantee a fair vote count, but the Democrats actively worked against one in Ohio.

Grassroots activists and volunteers in Ohio, New Mexico and elsewhere devoted many thousands of unpaid hours after the election to investigating the widespread belief that the election had been stolen. By contrast, the Democratic Party stood by quietly, often ridiculing them. Franklin County Chair Bill Anthony called them conspiracy theorists.

As more and more questions were raised about how the election had been conducted and how the votes were counted, the Kerry campaign directly attacked in the public media those who challenged the outcome. Specifically, its attorney Daniel Hoffheimer filled Ohio's airwaves with disparaging comments about those doing the precinct-by-precinct digging that had been expected of the Kerry Campaign. Election protection activists were mystified in particular by why the Democrats had hired a lawyer from the staunchly Republican Taft, Stettinius law firm to attack them.

As the challenges to the Ohio vote unfolded, the Democrats contributed very little money to the research that would confirm that, in fact, not every vote was counted, and that Kerry had actually won the election.

9. With a few exceptions, local, state and national Democrats lent virtually no support to hearings and investigations that revealed many of the irregularities, fraud and theft that defined the Ohio 2004 election.

When election protection activists convened public hearings so that those who had been disenfranchised could testify, they consciously included Democrat, Republican, Green and Libertarian voter rights activists on the hearing panel. But the Democratic Party regulars joined the Republican Party regulars in abstaining. Neither the Democrats nor the Republicans made an official presence.

Columbus, for example, has a Democratic mayor. When Congressman Conyers held hearings in the Columbus City Council Chambers, all three African-American members of the Columbus City Council did attend, while the four white Democrats did not. The mayor was also missing.

From the Ohio Legislature, only State Senators Ray Miller (D-Columbus), Teresa Fedor (D-Toledo), C.J. Prentiss (D-Cleveland), Larry Price (D-Columbus) and Mike Mitchell (D-Columbus), and State Representative Dan Stewart (D-Columbus), supported the statewide effort.

After Rev. Jesse Jackson got involved, the "democratic wing" of the Democratic Party became forcefully and effectively active. Rep. Conyers, Rep. Jesse Jackson, Jr. (D-IL), Rep. Jerrold Nadler (D-NY), Rep. Stephanie Tubbs Jones (D-OH), Rep. Dennis Kucinich (D-OH), Rep. Maxine Waters (D-CA) and others exhibited the concern and commitment many grassroots Democrats had hoped would come from John Kerry. Sen. Barbara Boxer (D-CA) made possible the unprecedented Congressional challenge to the Ohio Electoral College delegation that took place January 6, 2005.

But, overall, the mainstream Democratic Party, including the party organizations throughout the counties and states of Ohio, Florida, New Mexico, Nevada and Iowa and nationally, played no significant role whatsoever in challenging what happened in the states that swung the 2004 election. As mentioned, regular Democrats have, in general, been outspokenly hostile to the effort. The same has been true of the Kerry campaign.

10. The Democrats did not contribute significantly to the recount of the Ohio vote.

Secretary of State Blackwell resisted a recount in Ohio as best he could. He delayed certifying the official vote count as long as he could, narrowing the time for a recount, and pushing it past the date when the Electoral College delegation would convene.

It was the Libertarian Party and the Green Party (which was not on the ballot in Ohio) that raised the money and forced the recount to occur. Other than a few marginal "me too" filings, the Democrats made no significant commitment of money or effort to recounting the vote in the close, extremely suspect race in the state that cost them the presidency.

In August, 2005, with a third recount suit pending in federal court, Kerry threatened to pull out the last of his campaign's marginal support.

11. Kerry commented that he lost every precinct in New Mexico that had an electronic voting machine, but then did nothing about it.

In a conference call involving Rev. Jesse Jackson, co-author Bob Fitrakis and attorney Cliff Arnebeck, John Kerry commented that he understood that he had lost every precinct in New Mexico where the votes were counted with touchscreen DRE electronic voting machines. He said the presence of the machines trumped whether the precinct was Hispanic or white, Democratic or Republican, rich or poor.

But Kerry's knowledge that something was dreadfully wrong with the way votes were being counted in a crucial swing state did not move his party to investigate what might actually have happened in New Mexico. Quite the opposite.

12. In New Mexico, Democratic Governor Bill Richardson prevented a recount from occurring.

Grassroots election protection activists in New Mexico exerted tremendous effort, at great expense, to win a recount in that state. But they were fought off at every turn by Governor Bill Richardson, a Democrat. Among other things, the Richardson administration demanded huge financial resources from private sources before a recount could proceed.
As a result, New Mexico's votes in its close, bitterly contested and potentially crucial presidential balloting of 2004 remain un-recounted.

13. In Franklin County, Ohio, Democrats allowed Republican Board of Elections Director Matt Damschroder to hold his job in the face of major financial and vote manipulation scandals.

Prior to the 2004 election, Franklin County BOE Director Matt Damschroder, a right-wing Republican activist, accepted a $10,000 check from Diebold while in his office. Damschroder says he then mailed the check to the local Republican Party.

During the November election, Damschroder manipulated the distribution of voting machines, withholding many of them, to deprive inner-city precincts of their ability to conduct an efficient election. As has been widely publicized, the result was lines that lasted three to seven hours, and the disenfranchisement of thousands of African-Americans, most of them Democrats.

In July, 2005, Damschroder faced removal for having taken the Diebold check in his office. But Bill Anthony, the Democratic chair of the Board of Elections, praised Damschroder and the job he did during the November election. Damschroder was suspended for a month without pay, but kept his job. As of this writing, he is still Director of the Franklin County Board of Elections and is now stripping more than 100,000 citizens from the voter rolls.

14. In Hocking County, Democrats attacked a whistleblower and supported the Republican Director who illegally destroyed voter records and used her office to raise money for the GOP.

In Hocking County, the Board of Elections Deputy Director Sherole Eaton made public the fact that the Republican Director, Lisa Schwartze, had shredded thousands of pages of official documents. Schwartze did not have the permission of the Board of Elections to do so, as required by law. Schwartze further admitted to using her office to help raise funds for the Republican Party, which was also illegal. Eaton provided an affidavit alleging that a Triad technician changed out the County's hard drive on the central tabulation machine.

When Eaton blew the whistle, she was fired. A number of local residents and citizen groups came to Eaton's defense, demanding that she be reinstated. But the Democrats on the BOE supported Schwartze, and worked to prevent Eaton from getting her job back.

The Hocking County Democratic Central Committee asked both Democratic members of the BOE to resign; the BOE members responded that they were appointed by Secretary of State Blackwell and served at his pleasure.
The interchange led to the coining of a new phrase in Ohio politics: Democrats in Name Only (DINO).

15. In Warren County, Democrats never effectively challenged the "phantom Homeland Security Alert" that Republicans used to count the vote without media monitoring, resulting in a huge advantage for George W. Bush.

Democrats in Warren County allowed media to be shut out of the vote count due to a "Homeland Security Alert" called by local Republicans The vote count was then removed to an unapproved and unsecured warehouse. The source of the alert was never confirmed. The FBI continues to deny involvement in it.

The official Warren County tabulation, gave a large vote advantage for George W. Bush over his showing in 2000. It included a virtual statistical impossibility, in which more Democrats allegedly voted for an obscure candidate for the Ohio Supreme Court than for Kerry.

But the Democrats never effectively challenge the Warren County outcome, which provided Bush with a third of the margin by which he officially carried Ohio, and thus the presidency.

16. After the election, the National Democratic Party commissioned a study that confirmed many of the worst illegalities perpetrated during the election and the vote count and recount.

In June, 2005, the national Democratic Party issued a major study on the conduct of the 2004 election. The study joined Rep. John Conyers and concluded that "Jim Crow" discrimination had indeed been rampant throughout. It cited suspicious shortages of voting machines in inner-city precincts, problems with provisional and absentee ballots and a wide range of other irregularities that contributed to confusion, chaos and disenfranchisement on Election Day.

The study documented that throughout the state of Ohio, African-Americans were forced to wait, on average, nearly an hour to vote. White Ohioans waited just 15 minutes. (In Franklin County, the *Free Press* documented a 3 hour and 15 minute wait in Columbus's African-American wards compared to a 22 minute wait in the suburbs. One African-American precinct had a seven-hour wait).

The DNC study concluded that about three (3) percent of the state's voters failed to cast ballots due to long lines or other problems with the voting process. In the face of a total official vote count of more than 5.6 million, this represents about 170,000 votes, far more than the 118,775 margin of victory awarded George W. Bush. According to the survey, another one (1) percent of the vote was simply lost at the polling stations.

In other words, the official Democratic Party's study of the conduct of the Ohio election confirmed many of the worst racist abuses in the history of American presidential campaigns, at least outside the former Confederacy.

17. While the National Democratic Party's study of the 2004 election confirmed many of the worst GOP abuses, it concluded there was no party bias in those abuses, a virtually impossible conclusion.

The national Democratic study pinpointed a wide range of what it called "Jim Crow" abuses throughout Ohio's 2004 election, as had the Conyers Report. The Democrats acknowledged that black voters waited four times as long to vote as white ones. It also showed that some 170,000 citizens were deterred from voting by long lines and other problems, and that another 50,000-plus voters had their votes discarded outright.

But the Democrats then came to the astonishing conclusion that there was no difference in party affiliation among those who were thus disenfranchised, despite the fact that 83% of African-Americans voted for Kerry.

This could most kindly be termed counter-intuitive. African-Americans voted for John Kerry by margins of 8:1 and more. As the study states, they waited up to a statewide average of an hour to vote, versus fifteen minutes for whites, a majority of whom voted for Bush.

By all accounts, people who voted in suburban Republican wards breezed through. People who voted in inner-city Democratic wards were stuck in long lines.

The *Free Press* found 20% of the voters in one Franklin County African-American precinct waited in line to vote at least once without successfully voting. Richard Hayes Phillips estimates that up to 17,000 potential votes were lost for Kerry in Franklin County alone, an estimate that parallels similar research from the *Washington Post*.

So who, exactly, do the Democrats think those 170,000 citizens who turned away from the polls really were?

The Democratic study makes no mention of exit polls showing Kerry the victor, or of a wide range of questions relating to vote counts, Homeland Security alerts and other anomalies that prompted the U.S. Congress to question the Ohio outcome.

The Democratic report opens with a lament that the party lacked the resources to conduct an in-depth study of all the violations that apparently took place in 2004.

For a party and a candidate that spent nearly $300 million on a campaign while pledging to "count every vote," one must ask: "Why hasn't this promise been kept? Where did all that money go?"

Certainly those American citizens whom the Democrats will court to vote for them in 2008 will want an answer before they do so.

The authors' thoughts on the *DNC report* are in Wasserman & Fitrakis, "With a limp election theft report, Dems prove why they're unworthy," Freepress.org., June 28, 2005.

PART THREE:

WINNING BACK OUR DEMOCRACY

Chapter Eight:

For the Growing Election Protection Movement:
Honor Every Voter; Count Every Vote

1. Properly trained election observation and verification teams from the United Nations and accredited governmental and non-governmental organizations must be guaranteed access to all Ohio and U.S. polling stations.

Many of the worst abuses in Ohio 2004 and Florida 2000, among others, could not have occurred in front of non-partisan monitors and observers.

At very least, the American public and world community should demand a solid, reliable paper audit trail of all elections everywhere, even in Ohio.

The presence of neutral observers has long been standard in elections around the world. The United States has repeatedly gone to war in the name of bringing democracy to other countries. Woodrow Wilson most famously brought the U.S. into World War One to "make the world safe for democracy."

Part of that effort has always hinged on elections held up on the most intimate level to global scrutiny. To deny that same scrutiny within the United States, as happened in Ohio 2004, simply does not wash.

2. Access to polling places by partisan challengers must be banned.

The intrusion of partisan "challengers" in the Ohio voting process intimidated voters, made long lines longer and unjustly disenfranchised thousands. With non-partisan, neutral observers guaranteeing fair elections, there is no reason to allow party activists into the polling stations to harass voters. As Ohio 2004 has shown far too well, there is every reason to ban them.

3. There must be a Constitutional Amendment guaranteeing all American citizens the right to vote, and to have those votes fairly counted.

There is too much grey area remaining in the minds of those who would steal elections. It must be made clear that all Americans have the inalienable right to vote, and to have those votes reliably counted. After the nightmares of 2000 and 2004, it is clear that individual citizens need recourse to federal enforcement to guarantee this most basic right.

Congressman Jesse Jackson, Jr. (D-IL) has proposed a Constitutional Amendment guaranteeing all American citizens the right to vote. This Amendment should be approved. See his article "Fighting for a 'Right to Vote' Constitutional Amendment" in *Essential Documents*, p. 308. A thoughtful analysis of the need for a Constitutional Amendment appears in his *A More Perfect Union: Advancing New American Rights* (Welcome Rain Publishers: 2001).

4. There must be uniform federal standards for all elections, and those standards must support the right of all American citizens to vote, and to have those votes fairly counted.

As it stands now, when the United States conducts a federal election, the right to vote comes from laws in fifty separate and unequal states.

The states then conduct a separate election in each of their counties and precincts, with practices varying greatly from county to county and precinct to precinct. Ohio's 88 counties, for example, all have separate operating procedures and voting machines.

This may have made some sense in 1789, when the Constitution was adopted. But as we've seen in 2004, the enormous geographic and demographic diversity of the United States today make it too easy to manipulate national elections precinct by precinct.

So federal standards for federal elections must be outlined and enforced. But given the nature of today's Congress, the utmost care must be taken to make sure the federal standards actually encourage citizens to vote and guarantee their votes be counted, as opposed to actually making the situation worse.

5. Uniform federal election standards must include a guarantee that balloting is supervised by non-partisan commissions, not partisan Secretaries of State.

The travesties of Florida 2000 and Ohio 2004 must not be repeated. The idea of Secretaries of State administering elections while campaigning for partisan candidates running in those elections is patently absurd. As per Ohio's November 2005 proposed Constitutional Amendment, the practice must be banned nationwide.

6. The idea of universal, uniform paper ballots to be hand-counted must be considered.

Fierce debate now rages over how to reform the casting and counting of ballots. This is good: it means Americans are actively engaged in trying to preserve their most essential right.

We take no sectarian position on how to solve the problem of getting a reliable vote count in a national election. But we believe the idea of everyone casting a paper ballot and having them hand counted has merit, and must be discussed.

It is true that throughout US history, paper ballots have probably been as prone to tampering and theft as mechanical and electronic voting machines. But paper ballots are certainly preferable to electronic voting machines with no paper trail.

7. Electronic voting machines must be banned unless they provide a voter-verified paper ballot and audit trail, counted and recounted by independent, non-partisan citizen groups at the precinct level.

No matter what the nature of the overall debate on how best to cast and count ballots, there's no avoiding the fact that it makes no sense for any democracy to trust electronic "black box" voting machines which cannot be effectively audited, even at the point of casting the ballot.

Democracy's ultimate bad joke was played on Ohio voters who pushed the name of one candidate on a touchscreen only to see the name of his rival light up. To then have to leave the voting booth with no paper receipt guaranteeing where that vote actually wound up is to add insult to injury.

Federal legislation proposed by Rep. Rush Holt (D-NJ) and others in Congress and on the state level aimed at banning electronic voting machines without a paper trail must be passed.

What appears to be an excellent electronic system was invented by the late Athan Gibbs of TruVote. There may be others. But if the public insists on using electronic voting machines, somehow, somewhere, there is a way to make them reliably accountable.

That way must be found, and adopted, before the 2008 election.

8. All voting machines must run on open source code, transparent software that is owned by the public, not subject to proprietary restrictions imposed by owners or developers.

In response to an Ohio Open Records Law request, some counties in Ohio explained that they were incapable of making a full reporting because the software that ran their voting machines was proprietary to private companies. Those requesting information about this crucial election were referred to corporate executives who declined information based on the proprietary nature of the software.

This cannot be allowed to continue. If voting machines are to be used in future elections, they must be public-owned and their software must be open-sourced, transparent and available to public scrutiny.

9. On a federal basis, it must be made easier, not harder, to register to vote.

The moves by the Republican Party in Georgia, Indiana, Ohio and elsewhere to demand photo ID to vote, to throw up arbitrary barriers against voter registration drives, and to generally make it harder for young, elderly, poor and people of color to vote are all profoundly un-American.

At best these are cynical ploys for partisan advantage aimed at depriving certain Americans of their most basic rights. At bottom they are part and parcel of what can only end in dictatorship.

At the core of all of what America stands for is the most open possible process to allow as many citizens as possible to cast ballots and have them counted. Any federal regulations on voter registration, and all regulations within the states, must aim not at restricting the ability to get registered, but at making the process easier.

This means allowing registration forms to be filed anywhere in a state, regardless of where the newly registered voter will vote. It means giving maximum flexibility to workers in voter registration drives. And it means an absence of red tape designed only to exclude certain groups from the process for partisan advantage.

We could start by eliminating the GOP demands in Georgia and Indiana that voters present photo ID.

10. There must be no bans on the voting rights of ex-felons.

The ban on the voting rights of ex-felons is rooted in the racism of the post-Civil War former Confederacy. The white power structure there used this tactic as a ploy to keep black citizens powerless, disenfranchising hundreds of thousands of potential voters.

The ban also promoted the willingness of state governments to convict potential African-American voters of felonies, even if no crime had been committed, just to deprive them of their rights.

The situation is not much different today. In Florida 2000, the ban on the voting rights of ex-felons almost certainly decided the election for George W. Bush.

Among other things, the ban gives cynical state governments a way to deprive citizens who are NOT ex-felons from voting. In Florida 2000, threatening letters were sent to tens of thousands of citizens whose names merely resembled those of ex-felons, some of whom were from other states.

In Ohio 2004, Republican County officials sent out 34,000 letters to alleged ex-felons telling them they could not vote. But many of those letters went to people who had committed a misdemeanor, or no crime at all.

In both Florida 2000 and Ohio 2004, the attack on voters who were wrongly accused of being ex-felons helped swing the official outcome in both states and the nation.

Banning ex-felons from voting opens a Pandora's Box of disenfranchisement. For more than a century, partisan manipulators have been only too happy to open it. It can't go on.

11. A bi-partisan Constitutional Amendment proposed for the November, 2005, Ohio ballot, would create a non-partisan authority that would supervise redistricting of districts for the state legislature districts, and for U.S. Congressional districts in a fair manner.

The gerrymandering of Congressional districts in Ohio and around the nation has created a situation in which there are extremely few competitive races for U.S. Congress and for seats in state legislatures. The incumbent re-election rate has come to resemble those of the Politburo in the old Soviet Union.

A statewide Constitutional Amendment proposed by a wide range of citizen groups for Ohio's November 2005 ballot would create a non-partisan authority that would redistrict Ohio's Congressional and legislative districts in a fair manner.

12. The non-partisan redistricting authority would establish a mathematical system by which any alternative redistricting proposal would be evaluated and selected, including such factors as compactness and competitiveness.

Drawing Congressional and state legislative districts must be done by impartial, non-partisan commissioners.

Criteria for establishing the new districts would include proximity of voters to each other, thereby eliminating crazily contoured districts that infamously stretch for miles in tortured, unrelated patterns. In Texas, 2002, Congressman Tom DeLay (R-TX) created the poster children for such tortured, gerrymandered districts.

Revamped criteria would also include attempts to create districts in which party affiliations are closely divided, thereby yielding competitive races.

13. A Constitutional Amendment proposed for the November, 2005, Ohio ballot would require that elections be run by an executive selected by a non-partisan entity, rather than being controlled by a Secretary of State or other partisan official with a vested interest in the outcome.

A Constitutional Amendment proposed for Ohio in 2005 would put the administration of elections under the control of a non-partisan authority. This would remove the situation, made infamous in Florida 2000 and Ohio 2004, whereby elections are run by partisan elected officials, who also serve in dual capacities as co-chairs of presidential campaigns.

14. A Constitutional Amendment proposed for Ohio 2005 would restore limits on campaign spending, a good step toward starting to deal with the massive problem of campaign finance reform.

This Constitutional Amendment would limit individual contributions to political campaigns to $2000 (the lame duck bill passed by the GOP state legislature in December, 2005 raised that limit to $10,000, and allowed contributions from family members who are seven years old and up).

The amendment would also ban corporate donations to political parties.

The problem of campaign finance cuts to the core of American democracy. Without equity in the way money affects our elections, there is no real future for this republic.

Hopefully, the lessons of 2004 will lead to real change.

15. Other GOP election victories follow a pattern consistent with 2000 and 2004.

In 2002, in Georgia, incumbent U.S. Senator Max Cleland seemed safely on his way to re-election. He was substantially ahead in the polls right up to Election Day. But then he and the Democratic candidate for Governor, who was also ahead in the polls, lost by significant margins.

Right wing Christian activist Ralph Reed attributed the shocking Republican victories to late turnouts from church-based constituencies. But election protection advocates charged it was due to widespread voter fraud and theft.

In southern Ohio in 2005, Iraqi war veteran Paul Hackett launched perhaps the first gutsy anti-war campaign of the Bush era. Winning the Democratic nomination for U.S. House, Hackett plunged into a "safe" Republican district by labelling George W. Bush a "chickenhawk" who supported a war in which he was unwilling to fight.

Until late in the evening of the election, Hackett and his Republican opponent were running about even. But a "computer glitch" delayed the vote count in Clermont County, which had been rife was dubious vote counts and hampered procedures during the 2004 election.

Suddenly, the "glitch" was solved and Hackett went down to defeat, securing yet another House seat for Karl Rove and the GOP.

We wrote about Hackett's race in "Did the GOP Steal Another Ohio Election," which ran at Freepress.org August 5, 2005. Much has been written about the Cleland defeat, which election protection experts believe to be a poster child for GOP theft and fraud. Little has been said of the Hackett defeat, except that his 48% vote count in an extremely conservative Republican district should have served notice that the GOP could be in trouble in 2006, especially if the war in Iraq is still ongoing.

But the Cleland and Hackett defeats share a pattern with those of Al Gore and John Kerry: Democrats ahead or even in the polls, running strong into election evening, then suddenly a shift of fortunes, a computer malfunction, a glitch in the vote count...and....voila! another Republican victory.

Are these legitimate GOP victories? Or do they fit a larger pattern of manipulation and theft?

16. The 2004 experience in Ohio and around the United States should make it clear that democracy is hanging by a thin thread in this country.

In summer 2006, *The New Press* will issue a book of documents edited by Bob Fitrakis, Steve Rosenfeld and Harvey Wasserman on the 2004 election. By then we are certain more will have surfaced about what really happened to give George W. Bush the White House.

But it is clear that if the abuses outlined in this book remain uncorrected, and if the "reforms" the GOP has proposed for Ohio are enacted here and nationwide, the election of 2008 will indeed have been rigged even more thoroughly than in 2004.

With Ohio's 2004 fiasco, HB-1, the proposed HB-3, and the proposed Homeland Security Act as models for GOP action, the real question about the 2008 election is not "who will win the presidency?"

The real question is: "Why bother staging an election at all?"

17. There is a world of difference between losing an election and losing a democracy.

Americans in general have a hard time accepting the idea that an election can be stolen. They may also have trouble accepting how deeply endangered is our democratic form of government.

Stolen elections have long been a part of our history.

Even after two centuries, dispute still rages over who really won the election of 1800. The argument about electoral votes divided between Thomas Jefferson and Aaron Burr never ceases to fascinate historians.

But the more important question is whether John Adams would have won the election without the infamous "three-fifths bonus" given the slave states. The Constitution gave slave-owners an extra three-fifths vote for every slave they owned, even though the slaves themselves couldn't cast that vote. This was part of the price the slave states demanded for staying in the Union. Providing them that "bonus" was one of the reasons the Electoral College was established in the first place (why it remains in place after all these years is a failure of our system we all have to face).

Though few have paid much attention, John Adams always contended it was the three-fifths slave bonus that beat him in 1800, and he was probably right. Thanks to Garry Wills's recent "Negro President," the multi-dimensional discussion of that assertion has in many ways just begun.

We do know for certain that in 1824 Adams's son, John Quincy, cut a deal with the slaveowner Henry Clay to "steal" the presidency from Andrew Jackson, who won the popular vote.

We know that in 1876 the Republicans manipulated the electoral votes of Florida, Louisiana, South Carolina and one from Oregon to take the presidency from Samuel Tilden, who beat Rutherford B. Hayes by a quarter-million votes.

We know that in 1888, the Republican Benjamin Harrison took the presidency from the incumbent Grover Cleveland even though Cleveland won the popular vote. Cleveland took the presidency back in 1892.

We know that in 1896 Republican operatives under Mark Hanna stuffed ballot boxes from New York to North Dakota to take the presidency from William Jennings Bryan for Ohio's William McKinley. Hanna was the Karl Rove of the day, and Rove is well-known to be a great student of that epic election. Whether the vote count was really stolen is still being debated. But Hanna and his cohorts bragged far and wide that they had stuffed the ballot boxes and might well have considered killing Bryan had he won.

In 1960 the Democrats almost certainly stole Illinois for John Kennedy. Thanks to the manipulations of Mayor Richard J. Daley, the graveyards of Cook County came out en masse. But the great irony is—it didn't really matter. Though nationwide the popular vote was extremely tight, JFK won the electoral vote 303 to 219. Illinois's 27 votes could have gone to Richard Nixon and Kennedy still would have won the White House.

But in 2000, the infamous clash over Florida really did matter. There were several crucial ways George W. Bush and Karl Rove, with the help of Florida Gov. Jeb Bush, took that election from Al Gore, who won the national balloting by 500,000 vote. One was with faulty, incomprehensible ballots in heavily Democratic counties. Another was by using the disenfranchisement of ex-felons to bar at least 60,000 and probably more than 100,000 people from voting. Many of them were not ex-felons at all. Most were African-American who were voting roughly 9:1 for Gore. There's little doubt their votes could have easily overcome the tiny margin in Florida that gave the Republicans the White House.

In 2004, in Ohio, New Mexico, Nevada, Florida and elsewhere, the methods for stealing a national election have been far more complex and subtle, which may be one reason so many people have such a hard time accepting what was actually done.

As we've documented, the Republicans employed a staggering array of manipulations, dirty tricks and outright theft to take the election from John Kerry, who proceeded to roll over.

Our point in cataloging these tactics is not to mourn the loss of an election. The election protection community is long since "over it," especially since John Kerry was unwilling to fight to protect the rights of American voters who were disenfranchised en masse. Given its lackluster campaign and its non-existent attempts to safeguard the vote and the vote count, our commitment is not to somehow restore the Democratic Party to power.

As Jesse Jackson has said, we can afford to lose an election, but we cannot afford to lose the electoral process. We cannot afford to lose democracy.

So we worry that the kinds of things the Republicans have done in Florida 2000, in Georgia 2002, and in Ohio and elsewhere in 2004 will make it impossible for a candidate or party of true value to ever again get elected in this county. If what has happened to the electoral process as we've sketched in this book is even remotely true, and is allowed to happen again, American democracy is essentially over.

Part of the tragedy is that we have gone from a system that allotted votes for slaves who could not cast them, to a system where African-Americans have the right to vote, but are systematically denied it where those votes might really make a difference. Or they've been allowed to cast ballots, only to see them pitched in the trash.

Part of the evaluation of whether this election was stolen is wrapped into an analysis of who might have done it. It becomes necessary to ask: have we seen anything in the moral universe of George W. Bush, Karl Rove or Dick Cheney that would stop them from stealing an election for moral reasons?

One must also ask: do these people have the skills and structural power to pull off the theft of a national election? Or two of them?

The answer to the second question is a definite yes. The United States has been instrumental in overthrowing governments and rigging elections since the beginning of the last century. In recent years, George W. Bush's father, a former head of the Central Intelligence Agency, has been among the pioneers in rigging elections in Third World counties. The examples are legion. The means have become an art form.

In Florida 2000, the means were crude and obvious. In Ohio 2004, many highly sophisticated, easily concealed methods were used to skew the vote count. As we've shown in part, they were diverse, deniable and extremely effective. By any account of recent U.S. history, they were also well within the technical and financial reach of the people who run and advise the Bush/Rove/Cheney Administration.

What is profoundly different about the two stolen presidential elections of 2000 and 2004 is the impact they have had on America. The elections of 1800, 1824, 1876, 1896 and 1960 all had profound effects on our country's history.

But the successive thefts of national power in 2000 and 2004 have embedded into the American ruling structure an extremely aggressive two-term regime whose agenda for moving the US radically to the right is unprecedented.

Should the power of today's Republican Party become deeply enough ingrained in the genetic make-up of this country, and should its position be further entrenched through a permanently compromised electoral process, the America we all once knew will be gone forever.

Would it be within the moral universe of this administration to do such a thing as steal consecutive national elections? We leave that up to you.

Can this happen again? Will the elections of 2006 and 2008 be stolen?

We can only answer that as we see it now from central Ohio in the wake of the 2004 fiasco: all the pieces for yet another election theft are very much in place.

The methods are widening in their sophistication and range. The power of the party employing them has vastly deepened.

Will they do it again? Or will our democracy survive this unique and powerful storm?

The answer, dear reader, is up to you.

Bob Fitrakis & Harvey Wasserman
Columbus, Ohio
Fall, 2005

Harvey Wasserman

Professor Harvey Wasserman was raised in the Driving Park district of Columbus, where massive disenfranchisement marred the 2004 election. Today he lives about a mile away. He and his wife Susan have five daughters and two grandchildren. His ode to them is *A Glimpse of the Big Light: Losing Parents, Finding Spirit*.

Harvey has covered Ohio politics for forty years. He is author/co-author of a dozen books including *Harvey Wasserman's History of the United States*, first published in 1972 with an introduction from Howard Zinn. He has an M.A. from the U. of Chicago, and has taught history and journalism at colleges in Ohio and Massachusetts. His articles on politics, history and the ecology have circulated widely since the 1960s.

Harvey is known as a co-founder of the grassroots "No Nukes"/pro-solar movement, and as a leading advocate of farmer/community-owned renewable energy. He has served as senior advisor to the Nuclear Information & Resource Service and Greenpeace USA, for whom he spoke to 350,000 semi-conscious rock fans at Woodstock 2 in 1994. He is author of *Solartopia: The Future of Energy* and co-author, with wind pioneer Dan Juhl, of *Harvesting Wind Energy as a Cash Crop: A Guide to Community-Owned Wind Farming*.

In 1967 Harvey helped found the Liberation News Service and, in 1968, Montague Farm, one of America's longest-running organic non-profits, now home to the Peacemaker International organization. In 1979 he helped organize the massive "No Nukes" concerts in New York City. He's since helped organize grassroots movements in Ohio that: stopped the Perry 2 nuclear plant; prevented a regional radioactive waste dump; shut a trash burning power plant; and saved Franklin County's only wildlife refuge.

Widely known as a fiery radio/TV guest and public speaker, Harvey has addressed hundreds of campus audiences and public gatherings worldwide.

From www.harvey wasserman.com:

Harvey Wasserman's History of the United States (Introduced by Howard Zinn).

A Glimpse of the Big Light: Losing Parents, Finding Spirit (Introduced by Marianne Williamson).

Solartopia: The Future of Energy.

From Seven Stories Press: *The Last Energy War: The Battle Over Utility Deregulation.*

From CICJ Books (edited with Bob Fitrakis & Steve Rosenfeld):
Did George W. Bush Steal America's 2004 Election: Essential Documents

(written with Bob Fitrakis):
Imprison George W. Bush and *George W. Bush v. the Superpower of Peace.*

From www. danmar. us (with Dan Juhl):
Havesting Wind Energy as a Cash Crop: Guide to Locally-Owned Wind Power.

Films from Green Mountain Post (with Dan Keller): *Lovejoy's Nuclear War* and *The Last Resort.*

Bob Fitrakis

Bob Fitrakis is a Political Science Professor in the Social and Behavioral Sciences department at Columbus State Community College (CSCC), where he won the Distinguished Teaching Award in 1991. He was a Ford Foundation Fellow to the Michigan State legislature in 1975 and studied at the University of Sarejevo on scholarship in 1978. He has a Ph.D in Political Science from Wayne State University in Detroit, Michigan and a J.D. from The Ohio State University Moritz College of Law. He has also taught political theory at the University of Michigan-Dearborn and political science at Wayne State University and Oakland Community College.

His most recent book is "Did George W. Bush Steal America's 2004 Election? Essential Documents," co-edited with Harvey Wasserman and Steve Rosenfeld. He has also co-authored "George W. Bush vs. the Superpower of Peace" and "Imprison George W. Bush: Commentary On Why The President Must Be Indicted" with Harvey Wasserman. He is the author of "The Fitrakis Files" series of investigative journalism books. The first three titles are: "Spooks, Nukes and Nazis," "Free Byrd and Other Cries for Justice" and "A Schoolhouse Divided." Fitrakis also authored The Idea of Democratic Socialism in America and the Decline of the Socialist Party (Garland Publishers 1993).

Dr. Fitrakis currently serves as the Chancellor for Ohio and National Vice Chancellor of the International Association of Educators for World Peace.

Bob Fitrakis is the Executive Director of the Columbus Institute for Contemporary Journalism (CICJ), has published the Free Press since 1992 and acted as editor since 1993. The Free Press website, www.Freepress.org is currently earning international attention for its coverage of the 2004 election irregularities in Ohio.

Overall, Fitrakis has won 11 major journalism awards, including Best Coverage of Government from the Ohio Society of Professional Journalists.

In March 1994 Fitrakis served as an international observer for the national elections in El Salvador and in 1993, he visited Reynosa and Matamoros, Mexico as part of a human rights delegation to investigate conditions in the maquilladoras. As a result of the trip, he co-produced a video entitled "The Other Side of Free Trade" shown around the country at colleges and public access stations. He was an Associate Producer for Britain's Channel 3 production of "The 10 Greatest Heavy Metal Bands in British History." He is also a talk show host on Columbus' WVKO 1580AM, and a Near East Commissioner.

Co-editor, *Did George W. Bush Steal America's 2004 Election? Essential Documents*, (CICJ Books, 2005).

Co-author, *Imprison George W. Bush: Commentary On Why The President Must Be Indicted*, (HarveyWasserman.com, 2004).

Co-author, *George W. Bush vs. The Superpower of Peace*, (Columbus Alive Publishing, 2003).

The Fitrakis Files: The Brothers Voinovich and the Ohiogate Scandal, (Columbus Alive Publishing, 2004).

The Fitrakis Files: A Schoolhouse Divided, (Columbus Alive Publishing, 2003).

The Fitrakis Files: Free Byrd and Other Cries for Justice, (Columbus Alive Publishing, 2003).

The Fitrakis Files: Spooks, Nukes and Nazis, (Columbus Alive Publishing, 2003).

The Idea of Democratic Socialism in America: Eugene Debs, Norman Thomas and Michael Harrington, (Garland Press, 1993).

Did George W. Bush Steal America's 2004 Election? Essential Documents

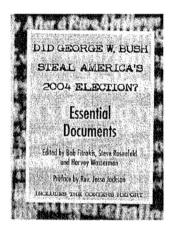

Edited by Bob Fitrakis, Steve Rosenfeld and Harvey Wasserman

Preface by Jesse Jackson
Includes the Conyers report: "What Went Wrong in Ohio?"
This collection of news analysis, legal documents, and sworn statements from hundreds of suppressed and disenfranchised voters may very well tilt the balance in revealing the election fraud in Ohio. These documents let the reader decide whether the 2004 presidential election was stolen.

$25 + $4 shipping

Other books by Fitrakis and Wasserman

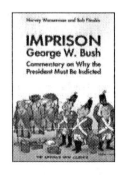

Imprison Bush

by Bob Fitrakis and Harvey Wasserman

Commentary on Why the President Must Be Indicted

A compilation of essays that read like a prosecutory indictment of the President. The *Free Press* editor and senior editor have thrown down the gauntlet.
$15

George W. Bush vs. the Superpower of Peace

by Bob Fitrakis and Harvey Wasserman
How a failed Texas oilman hijacked American democracy and terrorized the world

A collection of essays spanning the last three years by Harvey Wasserman and Bob Fitrakis charting these dark days of the Bush junta. But there is hope -- the Truth, and armed with the Truth, the forces of Peace will prevail.
$15

The Fitrakis Files books

by Bob Fitrakis

$15 - one book
$25 - two books
$30 - three books

Spooks, Nukes and Nazis

From the activities of the CIA, white supremacists to anthrax and buried radioactive waste, *Free Press* editor, political science professor and activist Bob Fitrakis has selected some of his most probing and insightful articles for publication in this book.

Free Byrd & Other Cries for Justice

On February 19, 2002, John William Byrd, Jr. was executed in Ohio's Lucasville death house for a crime that he insisted he did not commit. There was no physical evidence connecting Byrd to the murder, and the only direct evidence against him was the word of a notorious jailhouse snitch, himself a violent felon. Bob Fitrakis, award-winning investigative reporter closely followed the case to the end. This book includes his reports on the Byrd case along with other dispatches from the inner recesses of the prison-industrial complex.

A Schoolhouse Divided

Ohio's most feared journalist is going back to school! In his third volume of "The Fitrakis Files," award-winning investigative reporter and watchdog Bob Fitrakis sinks his teeth into the inequalities of public education. In a state where the education funding system has been repeatedly declared unconstitutional, Fitrakis finds urban school districts bitterly divided along racial lines, with up to 40 percent of the kids from affluent neighborhoods being shipped out to the suburbs, while the school board is mired in scandal and stymied by political jockeying. There are no winners at these schools — and the biggest losers are the kids, who are being taught all the wrong lessons about the importance of education.

The Brothers Voinovich and the Ohiogate Scandal

From a Cleveland construction company to county jail contracts to the Governor's mansion

---

Other books for sale

 **Leaked Secret Transcripts from Bush's Oval Office, 2002-2004 (satire)**

$15

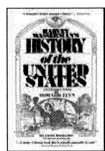 **Harvey Wasserman's History of the United States**

$15

 **Rotten to the Core 2 by Marty Yant**

To order: Freepress.org Online store
CICJ Books
1240 Bryden Rd.
Columbus, OH 43205

Essential Documents on the 2004 Election
767 pages. From CICJ Books/Freepress.org

DID GEORGE W. BUSH STEAL AMERICA'S 2004 ELECTION?

Essential Documents

Edited by Bob Fitrakis, Steve Rosenfeld and Harvey Wasserman

Preface by Rev. Jesse Jackson

INCLUDES THE CONYERS REPORT

**Coming in the Spring of 2006 from the New Press:
"What Happened in Ohio"
Edited by Bob Fitrakis, Steve Rosenfeld & Harvey Wasserman**

HARVEY WASSERMAN'S HISTORY OF THE UNITED STATES
Introduction by Howard Zinn

"A beautiful example of people's history…" from the introduction by Howard Zinn

"Harvey Wasserman is truly an original…" Studs Terkel

This much-loved cult classic from the Civil War to WWI is a mainstay for students and teachers in search of an alternative point of view—and a solid, exciting historic read.

From its legendary opening line—-"The Civil War made a few businessmen very rich"—to radical Populist farmers and Debsian socialist workers to the Greenwich Village parlors of Bohemian free lovers, your view of US history will never be the same.

By Harvey Wasserman*216 pages*$18.00*ISBN # 0-9753402-0-4*www.harveywasserman.com

SOLARTOPIA! THE FUTURE OF ENERGY

Climb aboard our sleek, green hydrogen-powered "Hairliner" as we fly half-way around an Earth of A.D. 2030 that has mastered the challenges of energy and the environment. Beneath us we see a post-pollution globe booming with the wealth and harmony of a revolution in sane power, one brewing since 1952, but finally in place.

From a pioneer advocate of sun/wind energy, *SOLARTOPIA!* joins *Looking Backward* and *Ecotopia*, *The Time Machine* and *Brave New World* as a classic in visionary thinking, this time on the life-and-death issue of sustainable energy and our ecological future.

By Harvey Wasserman*84 pages*$9.00*ISBN # 0-9753402-1-2*www.harveywasserman.com

A GLIMPSE OF THE BIG LIGHT: LOSING PARENTS, FINDING SPIRIT
Introduction by Marianne Williamson

"A knockout"…Kurt Vonnegut

"A song for the soul"…Bonnie Raitt

"Beautiful, elegaic, swinging, a long medium-tempo ballad with passages
of double time, like something Mingus might have played"…Ben Sidran

A unique, extremely powerful poetic excursion into grief and rebirth, loss and illumination, this soulful narration of the passing of beloved parents and the spiritual journey that followed is a rite of passage for all who seek. And a gorgeous symphony.

By Harvey Wasserman*164 pages*$18.00*ISBN#09753402-2-0*www.harveywasserman.com

www.harveywasserman.com*box 09683*bexley, ohio 43209* fax (614)237-0420

Printed in the United States
51297LVS00002B/367-438

9 780975 340288